chief yellowhorse lives on!

AND OTHER STORIES OF ARIZONA PLACES AND PEOPLE

Book Designer
MARY WINKELMAN VELGOS

Photography
CARLTONS' PHOTOGRAPHIC, INC., both covers
SCHNEBLY FAMILY, pages 35 (left), 177, 225
SHARLOT HALL MUSEUM/PRESCOTT, page 45
ROBERT CAMPBELL, page 149
FRANK ZULLO, page 241
LISA SCHNEBLY HEIDINGER, all other photographs

Book Editor
BOB ALBANO

Copy Editor
EVELYN HOWELL

Published by the Book Division of *Arizona Highways*®
magazine, a monthly publication of the Arizona
Department of Transportation, 2039 West Lewis
Avenue, Phoenix, Arizona 85009.
Telephone: (602) 712-2200
Web site: www.arizonahighways.com

First printing, 2003.

Printed in Singapore.

Library of Congress Catalog Number 2003104807
ISBN 1-932082-07-7

Publisher: Win Holden
Managing Editor: Bob Albano
Associate Editor: Evelyn Howell
Associate Editor: PK Perkin McMahon
Art Director: Mary Winkelman Velgos
Photography Director: Peter Ensenberger
Production Director: Cindy Mackey

ARIZONA HIGHWAYS
B O O K S

CHieF YeLLowHorSe LiVeS oN!

And Other Stories of Arizona Places and People

Lisa Schnebly Heidinger

dedication

For Tom Heidinger, my husband, who said: "You have a job; you're a
writer," even before it was true;

for Steve Bodinet, my friend, whose photographic advice was only a
fraction of the wonderful insights he's shared;

for Mike Schmidt, photographer and road partner extraordinaire,
who kept the "northern Arizona bureau code";

and for Phil Alvidrez, who, in hiring each, brought us all together.

author's note

The same irascible spirit that settled Arizona remains. Juan ("Chief") Yellowhorse made his mark with creative marketing on the Navajo Nation. He lives in my memory as an independent thinker who approached life with joy and a touch of wry humor. The other places and people and incidents described in *Chief Yellowhorse Lives On!* all hold a common thread: They stayed with me long after and had to be shared.

This book's essays came to me over many years. Some were planted in my childhood, such as traveling the road from Tucson to Nogales with my parents in our station wagon. Others got into my scrapbook of memories while I was a reporter, first for KGUN-TV in Tucson, then for KTVK-TV's northern Arizona news bureau. Some percolated out of vacation experiences with my husband and children.

My father, Larry, from whom I inherited the "going-in-the-car gene," joyously embarked on revisiting many of these sites, giving my 8-year-old son Rye a hand out of the quicksand at Lee's Ferry and helping 10-year-old Sedona earn her Junior Ranger badge at Pipe Spring National Monument. (My mother, Lee, offered most of her support over the phone from Tucson.) My husband, Tom, a co-worker whom I met at the Winslow prison when I did my first satellite live shot for KTVK, still pilots the great satellite truck around many of these places and understands the call of the road (what his father calls the "traveling bone").

By putting these 52 pieces together, I leave as many others out. Arizona is too vast, too steeped in things both powerful and odd, to be captured in a single sweep. But if we all contribute a puzzle piece, we add to the overall picture of this rugged, independent, delightfully absurd, majestic, and magical place we continue to encounter in new ways.

— Lisa Schnebly Heidinger
   Phoenix, March 2003

contents

A ponderosa
pine's snag
spears the blue.

the red setter in all of us

1 Snow brings it out — the red setter in us all. I may be walking carefully with measured, crunching steps, but inside I'm leaping, tongue out in a loopy smile, enjoying the different outdoors created overnight.

In parts of Arizona, snow pleasantly surprises you once a decade or so, but most of us still live only a few hours away from a good storm every winter. Many of us go to the mountains for a fix.

Between times, I forget some aspects of living with snow: how your nose goes on autopilot and runs from the time you hit your cold threshold until after you're back inside; how your fingers actually burn after you've scraped the car windows. But I also discover each winter, as if for the first time, the starry patterns of frost on that windshield before it's scraped; the hush that an insulated world acquires; the almost lit-from-within quality of a fresh snowbank.

Snow literally transforms the landscape. "Rough" and "jagged" no longer apply. Branches lose sharpness under undulating drapery. Edges become suggestions. Everyday objects now appear as artwork: a bicycle is a sculpture of softness, a car is puffy and vague. And when the sun comes, trees sparkle like a giant centerpiece sprayed with glitter.

The ocean may be very straightforward, but playing in the waves

Snow adds a brisk touch to Northern Arizona University's Old Main.

13

can be equipment intensive: sunblock, towels, sandals to get over the hot sand, maybe a boogie board. So it is with snow: Preparation really helps enhance the experience. We glove, we wind scarves, we buckle boots. Then giddy with anticipation, we go to become part of this new world done up in winter white.

And what a white! Midday, it makes you squint. Even under a cloudy sky, it is almost astringent in its whiteness. The most beautiful snowscape I've ever seen was in Flagstaff. I was driving very late at night and stopped at an unplowed intersection. The starlight illuminated the snow with almost phosphorescent brightness. I saw a skunk step delicately out onto the snow-covered road. His small body loomed starkly black, and his footprints made faint shadows as he walked gently across the pure whiteness of reflected starshine. I can see it still.

Anything powerful in nature has an opposite and equal dark side. When Mike Schmidt and I were the northern Arizona news bureau for KTVK-TV, winter storms meant horrifically long days spent documenting the good and bad news that snow brought. We got up before dawn to shoot video of schoolchildren waiting for the bus, invigorated homeowners shoveling driveways, and sagging awnings heavy with the night's snowfall.

Then we'd usually hit the highway, because storms inevitably brought accidents. Driving in snow meant making every movement gingerly, enduring the added stress of seeing ominous tracks where drivers less cautious had careened into embankments. Sometimes, the rollover still lay there, making our hearts shudder.

Every time I cross beneath the J.W. Powell Boulevard overpass at the south edge of Flagstaff, I picture the cab of an 18-wheel rig swinging gently above — one of the more amazing accidents we covered. The trucker lost control on Interstate 40 where the highway crossed over Interstate 17, and the cab jumped the guardrail. Torn off, the front axle fell to the roadway beneath, but fortunately, no one was below. The driver, probably more carefully than he did anything before or since, climbed out of the swaying cab and managed to scramble back onto the body of the truck to safety. With no one injured, the driver got a big kick out of seeing photographs someone dropped off for one-hour developing, even while the truck was still being rigged up to tow away.

We also realized over time that, while we loved the news truck's added safety of four-wheel drive, the vast majority of accidents we covered involved oversize and four-wheel-drive vehicles. It didn't take a rocket scientist to figure out that people in sedans and old compacts crept along, alert for black ice, while those in the sport utility vehicles reveled in a false sense of invincibility.

Driving in snow, while tension-filled, also reveals breathtakingly gorgeous views. The flakes swirl up to greet you and dance in wavy patterns across the asphalt. My father smiles when he goes over a cattleguard, because it tells him that he is out in rural country. I beam when I see a snowplow, because it means I'm in a winter storm.

At some point, true participation gets too chilly, toes stiffen from cold, and snow starts looking better as a spectator sport. Occasionally, the windows get magnificent frosty patterns. I always wanted to watch a snowstorm from one of the big chairs at the Flagstaff library, with a fireplace for contrast.

Storms develop their own personalities: sometimes rapid "corn" snow, almost granular, then slowing as the moisture builds a better snowflake, and heavier portions swirl and drift. Even later, roofs recycle fallen snow, letting it slide off in spectacular slow motion.

I understand why people who grew up in snow gladly relish living in parts of Arizona where they don't have to own a snow shovel. I sure understand why parents who have zipped coats, wrestled little hands into gloves, and tied hoods, only to undo and repeat the process endlessly during a day, would rather live in the desert and buy bathing suits year round.

But knowing all that can go wrong when driving in winter weather, I hope I never grow so aware of the risk that I forget to make at least one annual pilgrimage to a snowstorm, where the world is covered and gentle and brilliantly new.

Snow is one of nature's great gifts, especially in Arizona. Snow blesses us with water in disguise, bringing with it opportunities for games, making regular walks exhilarating, and giving us all a new place to live, without having to move.

holding the fort

2 Fort Lowell lingers as a leftover piece of Arizona history in a central Tucson park, surrounded by playground equipment and parking lots. Visible behind protective fencing, parts of the old adobe hospital building are protected from the elements by a large metal roof. You can see sections of room, rounded corners of eroding wall, dirt floors and doorways.

A cavalry bugler perpetually sounds a call at Fort Lowell Park's entrance.

Where 19th-century officers marched and Territorial doctors wrote receipts, we played hide and seek as children. A window between two rooms was "base." We would duck and crouch in the partitioned areas,

17

the excitement heightened by knowing this had been a building used a century before; knowing on the very spot I huddled quietly, a sick soldier may have had his head sponged with cool cloths by an orderly. Now, playing there seems like learning to climb on the Eiffel Tower or using old Picasso sketches as doodle pads.

But we didn't feel that way, any more than my father had worried about eroding northern Arizona's Sunset Crater volcano, when as Boy Scouts in the 1930s they were allowed to lope down the cinder cone's slope in preternaturally long strides. To us, Fort Lowell was just part of normal: a dirt-floored ruin for our games, as important but no more significant than the ice cream we sometimes bought on the way home.

Once heavy rains collapsed a section of the wall, and I found a scrap of newspaper with fragments of Spanish words on it. I viewed this as a message in a bottle from another time and puzzled over its possible meaning. Simply to hold this weightless bit of reality, a century old, and wonder whose hand touched it last fascinated me. A laborer, mixing adobe? An officer who threw it into a garbage pile, where it ended up getting caught between bricks when they were laid?

Eventually, good sense prevailed over recreation, and the ruin was enclosed in wire fences. Since we had just about outgrown playing hide and seek, we could be pleased with the preservation effort.

It seems Fort Lowell had always struggled to survive, from the time the military established it in the 1870s, located 7 miles outside of Tucson to shield the soldiers stationed there from the distractions of city life. The slipshod adobe buildings leaked; in true government fashion, fixing them would have cost more than building them had. And the fort wasn't in full use except once in the 1880s during the pursuit of Geronimo. Shortly after that, the army abandoned it.

One of the original buildings standing across from the museum is still inhabitable. A few stumps and corners of adobe are scattered nearby. My brother surprised us all by digging in our back yard almost a mile from the fort and finding a bayonet, which a local curator identified as belonging to the Fort Lowell era, probably lost during a drill or abandoned on a patrol.

The neighborhood around the fort is called "El Fuerte" in its honor and includes an old adobe church. After sitting smoke-stained and abandoned when I was young, leading children to tell of resident ghosts and dare one another to knock on the door, it has been restored and now hosts an annual Mass and assorted religious celebrations like weddings.

I run with my father through El Fuerte, streets that give way to bosque or cienega, thick with tamarisk, mesquite, weeds, and grasses that thrive from deep soakings during summer rains and subsist on high groundwater between them. We stitch a path along the riverbed's edge, ducking under low-growing branches to come out by the bridge — where bulldozers and earthmovers are scraping a section of desert raw, reducing the riotous tangle of brush to nothingness to support another building. Shaking our heads, and sorry to lose more natural land, we run over the Corbett Ditch, which wasn't named by its ancient Hohokam builers but by the pioneer who used it later. Just past that lies a beachhead of Fort Lowell's original adobe wall, like a baby whale separated from its pod. I put my hands against it, trying to figure out how to keep the old wild way intact in this hungry modern city.

But it dawns on me as I do so that a tribesman watching from a lofty outpost in the foothills while the fort was being built would have felt the same invaded outrage. What to me is appealingly antique was to him desecrating his homeland: laying out rigid rows of trees in militaristic order, erecting walls and fences over what had been rabbit and wildcat territory. Now it's nostalgia, but in its time, it was progress of the kind I curse.

If the rebuilt officers' quarters are open, it's fascinating to see the quaint relics from more than a hundred years ago: straight razors, papers in faded brown ink, short beds, and elaborately braided wool uniforms. Photographs show people who look like us, and yet different. (My daughter once said, "Mama, when I think of you as a little girl, I think you were in black and white.") To know that those people trod these paths is like a nail I snag my mind on. How did things look to them?

It's odd that the few women who lived in that barren outpost tried desperately to infuse some sense of civilization into the wilderness. Now we go out searching with equal desperation for some wilderness in all this civilization.

It all depends on which stop you board the anthropological bus. To me, the Fort Lowell ruins are good, modern apartment complexes are bad. To those long before me, the fort was the intrusion. I guess that's nature's way of making urban growth a little less painful: Each generation sees only so much of the big picture. I wonder, then, if the pendulum is only in mid-swing. Two thousand years from now, will the desert be without water again, and will someone gaze in wonder at the foothills scattered with empty shells of homes? In some cases, even harder than seeing empty spaces filled, would be seeing them gradually abandoned.

calling on the riordans

3 Touring the Riordan Mansion in Flagstaff can feel as if you're spying on Territorial life in 1904. Open to the public as Riordan Mansion State Historic Park, the 13,000-square-foot home, built with rustic log-slab siding for the Riordan brothers, adds the lone American Craftsman-style jewel to the State Parks crown.

A stone arch forms a sturdy entry way to Riordan Mansion.

Timothy and Michael Riordan built their fortunes as lumber magnates when huge ponderosa pine trees still forested the mountainsides. The Riordan brothers harvested some of those pines to build a double

21

home for their respective families, basically building mirror wings off each side of a massive common space that the families called the ball room, or sometimes the billiard room.

The Riordan brothers came to the then-small northern Arizona town of Flagstaff to help their brother Matthew with his lumber operation. Matt Riordan ultimately sold the business to them and moved on.

Marrying the Metz sisters, cousins to the well-known Babbitt family, Timothy and Michael occupied the top tier of local society. Their spacious home welcomed just about every prominent visitor to the Flagstaff area around the dawn of the 20th century.

Today, park tours begin in the mansion's visitors center, which includes touchable relics and family photographs and documents. The visitors center occupies what was originally the Riordans' six-car garage, designed by a skeptical architect who included rein rings at intervals, for when the horseless carriage proved to be a passing fad.

Since Michael Riordan's wing remained occupied until 1985 by his daughter Blanche, only Timothy's wing has welcomed the guided tours. Michael's home was finally opened recently for short unguided visits. Above the back door, a tilted snow gutter makes sure the runoff benefits the kitchen garden. Timothy's fascination with engineering and innovative details like this probably played a key role in the home's design.

While the actual cost to the Riordans is not known, building the mansion today probably would run into the millions of dollars, starting with the huge log slabs, curved and rough with bark, siding the entire home. The back door leads from the servants quarters into the ball room, which also served as a den for both families. The room's billiard table weighs as much as a large pickup truck, and players kept score on a wire stretched overhead by sliding wooden beads across.

Flanking the huge fireplace rise one of the home's more spectacular but fragile features: illustrated windows that exist only here and in a rare few museum and private collections. Created with a technology now lost, the original windows bonded John K. Hillers' photographs of the Grand Canyon and other Arizona sights with silvery panes of glass. Once, breakage, fungal damage, and chemical deterioration threatened the images of ancient rock houses and Indian faces. Now, though, the public can see daylight glowing through brilliant restorations while still marveling at original panels displayed in the west wing.

On the way upstairs you pass a small chapel, hinting at the strong Catholic and civic roles the Riordans played, including raising construction funds for the grandly gargoyled Nativity Church downtown.

Servants occupied the back of the second floor, in what were roomy quarters for their time. The fragile wire hangers and eggshell linens still sit ready for use. The guest room next door has a fireplace to make sure visitors knew that, while they might be in a harsh territory, they didn't have to be uncomfortable. Michael Riordan designed some of the furnishings, which were crafted from walnut brought up from Oak Creek Canyon.

Dominating the center hall upstairs is the odd air circulator — an idevice Timothy included in his house plans for the family's summertime comfort. Waist high and big as a rowboat, the slatted space allowed hot air from the lower floor to escape through open skylights on warm summer afternoons. (Timothy's daughters apparently found a further use: drying their freshly washed hosiery.)

Timothy's older daughter Mary was immortalized when he named the lake he had dammed and filled just outside town after her. A belle and socialite in a town where competition would not have been stiff, Mary enjoyed an elegant upbringing, including a storybook wedding captured in a photograph displayed in her room. The room connects to her mother's. A photograph shows Caroline, a famous beauty even at age 60, as radiant and elegant as many women much younger yearn to be. One of her dresses shows how delicately built she was.

Timothy, on the other hand, was a robust and rousing character. His room, connected to Caroline's by a shared bath, is full of athletic gear, including a pith helmet and golf clubs. He loved taking visitors to the

Hopi Indian Reservation, and a photograph shows his daughters wearing their hair in the distinctive butterfly style of unmarried Hopi girls.

Photographs in Anna's room show a woman who was more interesting than lovely, with clear arresting features. On a dressmaker's stand hangs a favorite dress she insisted on wearing by adding ruffles as she grew taller — an indication of a woman who could afford to indulge her preferences. Sadly, her privileges were short-lived. When she was about to be married, at age 26, Anna attended a weekend picnic with family members. She went upstairs to rest afterward and woke up the next morning paralyzed from polio. She died a few days later.

The same day of Anna's death, in the other wing one of Michael's sons also died from polio. What a somber house it must have been, two of the bright young generation cut down suddenly and randomly within 11 hours of each other.

Back downstairs, the kitchen is set up with a butler's pantry containing ingenious drawers that open into the pantry on one side or into the dining room on the other, keeping utensils close at hand. A floor button worked the bell in the kitchen to summon kitchen help; glancing at the call box showed whether a servant was needed in the kitchen or another room similarly wired.

One of Timothy's designs makes his dining room slightly different from Michael's. Its football shape, with a matching table. meant no one blocked anyone else's view during a meal. Why this hasn't caught on, I don't know.

The home's foyer served as Caroline's music room. Once, on a tour, the guide let my mother play an old tune on her piano. With her pale hair and gentle touch on the keys, it was easy to picture her as the hostess charming the gathered guests.

Timothy's study has slim slanted storage for blueprints, like a sea captain's quarters had for maps, and a stucco corner fireplace. The study leads to the living room, which boasts a whimsical swing in the middle of the room. In the summer, it looked out on the courtyard garden at the front of the home; during snowy times, it could be turned around to face the fireplace. Some of the family's original Stickley furniture is here, along with tufted velvet window seats that make you want to choose a book from the shelves and settle in for an afternoon.

The lower floor of Michael's side of the house is now open to the public for short visits. The contrast in detail is fascinating: While both wings use stained glass, the shapes and colors of the windows are different. Michael added on a sleeping porch for his much larger family.

Some like to say ghosts still linger, that the scent of cigar smoke wafts from around the billiard table and that the figure of a woman appears near Anna's room. Walking through the house makes it easy to wish for the ghosts. So much of the family exists in the furnishings that the personalities seem too vivid to be gone. Timothy, regaling visitors with tales of Paul Bunyan's baby shoes (he had them made). Or Caroline, resting on her daybed with her impossibly small corset loosed. Mary and Anna, pausing in the upper hall, giggling about a boy from school. Visiting the house is the next best thing to visiting the family.

arizona's river road

4 Okay, it doesn't have the plantations and live oaks you'd see along Louisiana's River Road — Arizona may look less like the Old South than just about anywhere. But our "River Road," State Route 95 paralleling the Colorado River, displays a charm many Arizona residents and visitors never see.

When heading west on Interstate 10, for those of us who make the annual summer pilgrimage to California, to turn north before reaching Quartzite feels strange. Make that turn though, and you pass through Bouse and Parker, whose economies seem to rely on RV parks. In Bouse, a store's sign says "The A & C Whatever Shop." I can picture owners either so blasé that "whatever" is a philosophical statement or so excited that they sell whatever catches their fancy. And in Parker, Coffee Ern's with its big pink coffeepot sign was my favorite.

The Arizona California Railroad also headquartered in Parker. Its motto, "Where Safety Is A Way of Life," is emblazoned on the side of a trainyard building. As good a way of life as any, I suppose. Curiosity led me to search the Web for more information. The route goes into California past Needles and to Wickenburg for its eastern hub. There was no mention of passenger load.

If you want to sound terribly bright, remark to anyone with you

Lake Havasu forms the centerpiece of a town.

that Parker was named for General Eli Parker, an esteemed Iriquois Indian who fought with Ulysses S. Grant during the Civil War. He was the Commissioner of Indian Affairs when Congress established the Colorado River Indian Reservation near Parker in 1865.

Along the River Road you get flashes of the water between stretches of landlocked asphalt. Where you cruise alongside the Colorado, the scenery seems to mix California's Palm Springs and the Vermilion Cliffs of northern Arizona. The craggy red rock formation, with rugged spires over the familiar slope of talus you see around the Grand Canyon area, is pure Vermilion Cliffs, but the palm trees, homesites, and golf courses evoke Bob Hope Drive. It's an unusual hybrid, and makes me glad the Grand Canyon is as rugged and unforgiving as it is to human traffic. Any flat land, and the Canyon would have been zoned for residential, sure as shootin'.

Some of the geography belongs to the River Road alone. An expanse of river reeds glowed around one bend, reminding me of Sting's song "Fields of Gold." There are tumultuous gnarled mountain passes the color of gingerbread. Smack dab in the middle of those are a few unexpected spots of deep gray that appear to have wandered far from home. They would recognize the Canyon's volcanic Inner Gorge formations as distant cousins.

Watercraft leaving white tails plume across the Colorado River. From the 1850s to 1870s, paddlewheel boats churned up and down this stretch, to as far as what is now Lake Mead, carrying cargo and some passengers. The river beckons, cool and blue, but anyone who has been here in the summer knows that "cool" is relative. When it's 118 degrees on land, that little breeze you get on the water passes for relief.

Then of course comes Lake Havasu City, which enterprising chainsaw millionaire Robert P. McCulloch Sr. virtually created from so much sand and grit (of the determination kind). He went shopping in Europe for a landmark that would attract tourists, and after being denied the Eiffel Tower and the Tower of Pisa, he was fortunate enough to happen through London when a new bridge was needed to bear modern traffic. So the old London Bridge (dating from the 1700s) came to Arizona, dismantled and carefully numbered, brick by brick. Once the bridge was in place over the sand, McCulloch dredged a mile-long channel for the Colorado to flow under it. (Two interesting bridge facts I can pass along: There is a tunnel inside it; and if you look at the bridge from downstream, you can see where small sections were cracked off by a German plane downed in a World War II dogfight over London.)

Because this iconic bridge is the town's centerpiece, London decor dominates. From the dragons overlooking the tourist area to lions rather absurdly spitting into a fountain, you are reminded why you have come. A classic red phone booth and lots of Union Jacks complete the look.

Lake Havasu City has expanded like mad since the London Bridge's dedication in 1971. The mayor quoted a population of 40,000 that swells to 70,000 in the winter, when snowbirds migrate to the sunny shores of Lake Havasu.

Spring break season and summer holiday weekends bring the rowdier migration of the college set. In its heyday, this was a law enforcement officer's nightmare, especially where revelers could step from boat to boat in Copper Canyon, partaking of many dubious substances. Now with universities staggering their spring break schedules, things are tamer and less terrifying — or less fun, depending on your perspective.

After stopping at Shugrue's for a piece of coconut cream pie so luscious I've thought of it every day since, I reversed my path down the River Road. Missing the turn to I-10 at Vicksburg was the best road I never drove, because it brought me to a highway previously not taken. Besides the charm of knowing I now was somewhere I'd not traveled before, I got to drive through Hope, Arizona, and then past the sign that informed me I was now Beyond Hope.

An overcast day made the scenery brighter against the gray sky, and stray cotton fibers, apparently dropped from trucks after harvest, decorated the roadside like artificial snowdrifts for the holiday season. Almost no traffic came past. Looking at the homes, scattered in fits and starts, I thought one wouldn't have to go to a foreign country to meet someone with a radically different life experience. Here in Arizona were people who have no supermalls, no traffic jams, no mini-mart on the corner for milk in the middle of the night. And yet, we surely share some common culture: They would see the same celebrity gossip on cable television and in magazines, buy the same brands. I wished there had been a church social, so I could meet some of the residents of these very independent dwellings.

Turning south at Salome brought me back to I-10. I've been to the River Road in the summer, and I've been in the winter, and winter is better. When not obsessed with one's own overheated, sweating self, it becomes easier to see this remote, rugged section of Arizona where commerce has doggedly dug in and made the land blossom with RVs. I am impressed with Mr. McCulloch, who combined the magic trinity of money, determination, and luck to bring a city into being. I guess if you build the London Bridge, they will come.

why rye?

5 We swear we won't turn out like our parents; at least we will avoid their quirks that drove us craziest when we were kids. But like a child who was spanked grows up to be a spanker, I have visited upon my children one of the corniest aspects of my own childhood: theme names.

Sure, I can see how when Larry Schnebly dated Lee in college, it charmed them to think of a bunch of little matching "L's" running around. However, once they were married, they could have shaken off that notion before my siblings and I came along. But no. Laurie Lee was

Motorcycles line up in Rye's morning sun.

31

followed by Lisa, then the boys, Lindsay and Lyle. Because my parents ran out of energy long before they ran out of names, pets through the years were Leilani, Lasagna, London, Lolly, Locket, Libra, ad nauseum, until my mother brought home one Christmas what would be the last puppy and announced she was sick of it — this time, a name with no "L." No el. Get it? Christmas? Noel at least wasn't embarrassed about it, as I was about the multiple L syndrome. We're people, not mascots, I huffed. Having a little fun at the children's expense, weren't they?

Well, with chagrined hindsight I can see now that while I cringed, the concept was already seeping so deeply into my genetic pores, it could not be purged; not even by plans I had of naming children Jade and Joshua and Cypriana. I had fallen for the "theme thing," only with a twist: Arizona towns.

The first felt inevitable: When Tom and I found out we were having a daughter, naming her Sedona pleased us. After all, the town was named for my great-grandmother, Sedona Schnebly, Tom had proposed at a Schnebly Hill Road overlook, and we'd been married on Oak Creek's banks at the Sedona resort, Los Abrigados. Our daughter Sedona would be the first in our family since the other Sedona. My father was thrilled to be not only Sedona's grandson, but now Sedona's grandfather.

So, fine. When we find out I'm pregnant again, with a boy, I suffer from Theme Name Syndrome far worse than from morning sickness.

"Prescott," I say to Tom. "After all, we had our first dinner together there." He considers.

"The other boys would call him Prissy."

"Then Winslow!" I suggest. "We met there, after all!"

"They'd call him Winnie."

I get out the road map and start perusing. A second girl would be Greer, because then we'd have daughters bearing the names of two of the state's loveliest spots. (Tom wouldn't have considered Vermilion Cliffs Heidinger.) Running a finger up the Beeline Highway, I find Rye. Rye Heidinger. Strong, uncomplicated, without ruffles. The name passes my acid test of sounding as if it could belong to either a river runner or an attorney. I pitch it to Tom, who considers it.

"Rye. Well, that is where the Harley Davidson junkyard is."

My brother Lyle says it passes his test for a boy's name, which is to think about how such a guy would act if you threw up in his car. Someone named Rye would take it in stride, he told me.

So we decide he will be Rye Schnebly Heidinger, in order to feel some connection to Schnebly Hill Road, my great-grandfather's proudest work. When we go public with the name, the jokes start.

"How about Tuba City?" snickers a friend. "Or Ajo?"

"Bullhead Heidinger," says a coworker.

"You could call him Casa Grande . . ." or ". . . Window Rock . . ." or ". . . Cornville." Each suggestion was accompanied by a burst of laughter, as if by then we hadn't thought of everything from Kingman to Thatcher and in between.

Rye was born, and that was the end of our childbearing years. We did acquire a desert tortoise named Toltec, but he went to the Great Desert in the Sky. Later, a great white standard poodle (let us hasten to add he does not get a foo-foo cut!) moved in and became Happy Jack.

So it made sense to take a Name Tour. We started up the Beeline Highway and made it to Rye for lunch. Our boy Rye was a little startled about how very, very small "his" town was. We pointed out the Rye Creek Bar and Grill and were fortunate to be able to order Ryeburgers for lunch. We met the duo who played guitar at the Rye jam session, and they signed a poster for our Rye. Mollified by the repetition of "his" name, if not the scope of the town, Rye carried his souvenir to the car.

Next stop, Happy Jack. Rye felt a little better that the dog's namesake forest settlement was even more elusive than his in terms of finding a main business area: a lovely lodge and a Forest Service station.

We snapped a photo to show the dog and stayed the night in Flagstaff. The next morning at Macy's, the kids had peanut butter and jelly sandwiches the size of their heads, and we wound up the tour in

Sedona. Here we posed our daughter by a city limit sign as we had posed Rye by his highway marker. Visiting the willow trees at the Poco Diablo resort and the Tlaquepaque chapel, I was thinking that while Sedona is most obviously picturesque, it depends on what pictures you want. Sorry we hadn't also had a daughter named Greer and a son named Cameron (great names, longer tour with fantastic scenery) we headed home.

At that point, Sedona piped up from the back seat with the question I'd been subconsciously dreading since either learned to talk:

"Mama," she said, "what is it with you and Arizona towns, anyway?"

I can't really explain it, I said, and then asked them the best part of the trip, expecting to hear about how it felt to see their names on big green highway signs.

Rye said, "When we pretended to be Pokémon in the field with bugs by Happy Jack."

Sedona said, "When Poppa bought us the books with stickers in Flagstaff."

We may all travel in the same car, but each one's journey is different.

a pause on schnebly hill road

6

When it took four days to get from Oak Creek Canyon to Flagstaff, creating Schnebly Hill Road made sense. It cut the trip in half.

Now, if traffic is good on the switchbacks and you can get to Flagstaff in an hour, Schnebly Hill Road only makes sense if you're in it for the journey rather than the destination. It's 12 miles of lurch, jar, bounce, and rattle as the rocks and rain hollows have their way with your car. (Nevertheless, some of us Schneblys make it a point to baptize every car we buy with a trip down the road.)

Larry Schnebly, right, pauses along the road built by his grandfather, T.C. Schnebly.

35

The road is named for my great-grandfather, Theodore Carlton Schnebly, or T.C., who brought his wife, Sedona, to settle along Oak Creek in 1901. Besides applying for the first post office, he was one of a group of men who donated $300 each, to be matched by the Coconino Board of Supervisors, for the purpose of building that road.

Schneblys, Thompsons, Loys, and Foxes were some of those involved, and George Babbitt gave the county's approval. Kel Fox, whose father owned a ranch on Schnebly Hill Road for years, remembers T.C. supervising the road crew.

Following animal trails, the men wrested the road from sandstone bluffs and hillsides tangled with growth using what my father calls Mormon scrapers: wide sheets of curved metal with flat bottom rims and handles so a man could walk one behind a horse.

Starting at the base of Schnebly Hill, my dad points out where Uncle Billy Wallace lived in the early days. Wallaces and Schneblys were friends; daughter Margaret Schnebly married son Stanton Wallace. Uncle Billy intrigued the local children because of a metal plate in his head, inserted in rudimentary surgery after he was wounded as one of Teddy Roosevelt's Rough Riders in the Spanish-American War.

"The cold in Flagstaff made the plate hurt, so he moved down here," my father remembers. "A nice, gentle man."

From that point, you see the old road wind in a ribbon far ahead. Engineers re-routed that in 1930 "because a horse can turn a lot sharper than a car," my dad says.

Bear Wallow is next, on your right: a side canyon about a mile up the road with silty sand coming down. Back when Jesse Howard earned the nickname "Bear" for his skilled hunting, and pioneer Richard Wilson was killed by a bear in Oak Creek, the name had more relevance, but it's fun for children to play with a heightened sense of possibility in the fine dust or rain runoff there.

Another mile up is where Mantel Rock shows: Between two taller formations, it's a square that could be a fireplace. T.C. was up in Flagstaff when severe rains carved out the center hearth section that gives it the fireplace appearance. When he came back down, the raw red hollow was newly exposed, with a wide swath of talus below showing where the rockslide had taken out trees and dirt. He wished he could have witnessed the buckling and splitting himself.

Merry-Go-Round Rock stands about 5 miles up. My father remembers a movie crew using ropes to painstakingly lower covered wagons over the concentric whorls of ancient sand dunes. ("Nobody did that in real life, but it illustrated pioneer hardship very effectively for the movie.")

At the 6-mile midpoint, Schnebly Hill Road Vista offers a panorama of the canyon. It was on this windy bluff at sunset many years ago that Tom Heidinger turned to me and said, "I love you, and in front of God, and all your ancestors, I'm asking you to be my wife." After I accepted, we downed the last sips of wine from our cups and, without speaking, lofted them up, out, forward, circling end over end as they fell into the wilderness below, where eventually the clay would turn to ground once more. Every time I come here, I remember that graceful arc of goblets whose last use was the beginning of a marriage.

Past the overlook, the road levels out considerably, giving way to the piñon, juniper, and finally, ponderosa pine trees. About 4 miles past the overlook is where the Fox family ranch, Foxboro, stood for years. Kel Fox said his father created a boarding school that lasted for 10 golden years in the 1930s. He recalls how many young men traveled through and asked for a few days' lodging in exchange for work. One, however, couldn't seem to stay on a horse, no matter how gentle the mount.

"So he couldn't be a great deal of help," said Kel. "But he had a camera, and he did send us some pictures. I've always wished I knew what happened to those; it wasn't until later that the name Ansel Adams meant something."

Foxboro's buildings have been leveled; only the dam remains that Frederick Fox built to store water.

From here it's a brief drive to the top. My father plans to run the entire length of Schnebly Hill Road for his 75th birthday. T.C., who didn't believe in slowing down as you aged, would approve.

T.C. always got his walking canes off Schnebly Hill Road; he found the manzanita that grows thick and twisted to be so strong he would pull it out of the ground rather than attempt to cut it off.

Once when my father was young, he and his dad, Ellsworth, accompanied T.C. on a cane hunt.

"My dad looked over at one point and said, 'For cryin' out loud, Dad, what do you think you're doing?' T.C. had scrambled probably 25 feet down a cliff that seemed almost sheer. He'd seen a piece of manzanita he wanted. And he got it."

T.C. also harvested yucca up here for Sedona to use in making soap, and he later carved century plant, or agave, stalks into slices that he gave away as pincushions. Early visitors to Sedona often found T.C. downtown. Lonely after his wife of 50 years died, T.C. introduced himself to strangers and told them about the area or helped them plan hikes and day trips. To the women, he would offer the century-plant pincushions, soft in the center with the sturdy outer skin with his name burned into the underside.

I think it's significant that when T.C.'s estate was settled, his net worth came in at only several hundred dollars, even though he had at one time owned the 80 acres that now hold Los Abrigados and Tlaquepaque. He did not define success in financial terms.

In our family, T.C.'s legacy includes the bromide, "Count the day lost you don't draw blood." I explain to a child staring horrified at a fresh scrape that T.C. meant you were at least doing something fun or useful, instead of sitting around.

The most evocative family story about T.C. tells of when a catastrophic hailstorm flattened his crops in Boyero, Colorado. While the family sat stunned in the kitchen, contemplating the dire financial consequences of the battered fields, T.C. walked in and looked around at the doleful faces.

"Well, let's not just sit here," he urged. "Get some buckets — we're going to collect that hail and make ice cream!"

My father adored his grandpa and remembers him as affectionate, encouraging, and independent. We have a photograph of T.C. as an old man, busy at his desk. I wish we had a similar photograph of his son Ellsworth, who I remember also being busy at his desk a great deal of the time. And it isn't too late to take that photograph of my father in a similar pose, using his computer instead of his father's typewriter or T.C.'s fountain pen.

T.C. Schnebly was a man of graciousness and grit. He extended himself to those he loved and those just newly met. A dawn-to-dusk worker, he measured life in conversations, not dollars.

The headstone in the pioneer cemetery says about T.C.: "He lives on in Schnebly Hill." It's a good legacy: The road is basic and without frills, but if you're willing to put in the work, the payoff comes in the driving skills and the view. If you decide to stop and hike there, you might even get to draw blood.

passing the prison

7Scenery doesn't exactly compete for space on the road from Phoenix to Oracle. Only a part of it, I suppose due to county lines, is the Pinal Pioneer Parkway, and many people do take this route (State Route 79) to Tucson, even though it's a little longer than Interstate 10, because the vegetation and land are more interesting. (Which isn't saying much.)

So driving with my children, I seized on the state prison at Florence as something to point out. Maybe there would even be a teachable moment here. I told them that their dad sometimes comes here for Channel 3 news to cover executions, and I explained what those are. I showed them the Blue Mist Motel, which some say was named for the cloud of chemicals that used to be released when the gas chamber was used. The guard towers and seeming miles of barbed wire awed them. We even took a picture.

Coming back, we passed the prison from the south and noticed something we hadn't seen before: the Prison Arts and Trades Outlet.

"Let's stop!" both back-seat passengers shouted. I pulled in, intrigued by the low wood building with its sign: "Denim Jackets, $5." Other than a few clothes, everything sold here was made by prisoners in the state corrections system.

The Prison Outlet displays some of its goods.

41

Inside it evokes the rather specialized roadside curio shops that used to sprout along Route 66 in its heyday. There were lots of leather items: wallets, purses, and glasses cases. Jewelry glittered from tiny ziplock bags and wall displays. Clothes hung down the center, and t-shirts filled shelves. The kids wandered up and down aisles, bringing me their favorite finds: a mesh laundry bag, a wooden box, and a mancala game board.

I was deciding that next year I would purchase Christmas gifts here. It would be a good way to reinforce positive behavior — these are people who could be spending their time lifting weights to be more dangerous when they get out of prison, instead of applying acrylic paint to cardboard and enclosing rocks as game pieces. So I agreed to buy the mancala board for the family and got out my $9.95.

Behind the counter, decorative license plates bore brave, state-proud messages. My favorite was the most poignant: "W8 4 me." Of course, the person driving the car doesn't need waiting for — it's the one behind bars who won't get anywhere near the vehicle. Still, it stayed in my mind.

As I paid, I asked if it was possible to find out who made the game we were buying. The clerk checked her inmate number list and said it was Rusty Morris.

Rusty Morris.

Of all the thousands of inmates in Arizona's prisons, this magenta-flowered board was crafted by the only one I knew personally.

I told the children and the clerk the story.

Rusty is serving a life sentence for the murder of his wife, Ruby. But 25 years ago, he was the oldest son of a family I joined for Thanksgiving. Newly dating the youngest son, I was anxious to make a good impression on a house full of people.

Over the next few years, I saw a fair bit of all of them, on holidays and weekends. Maxine, the mother, may still be the most maternal person I have ever known. She could not do enough for her children and grandchildren. Maxine cared nothing for gifts on holidays and wanted only to be remembered on Mother's Day. A tireless cook, server, and hostess, she seemed to live solely to make sure that everyone was fed, comfortable, and happy.

Rusty was an accountant and did well enough that I remember Ruby proudly displaying gifts of jewelry on special occasions. He did my taxes for several years, and it was Rusty who never lost patience when coaching me as I tried to learn to water ski. How many dozens of times did he say, "Okay, let's try it again," until I finally remained standing behind his power boat?

So when I read 10 years ago about a Rusty Morris being tried for murder, and saw Ruby's name as the victim, I went to see if it was the same man I'd known and liked.

It was, and I will never know how he survived the day of his preliminary hearing. He had to endure the telling of not only how prosecutors believed he had killed his wife, driven her body to San Diego, and put her on the boat that he then burned and sank. He also had to hear about two of the children he had raised as his own having been fathered by someone else.

He was convicted by a jury and is serving his sentence.

The whole thing brought home to me the fact that the world is not divided cleanly into purely good and purely evil people. I did a death-row interview with a murderer who started to use a bad word and apologized. We are all an amalgam of our finest and weakest traits. I have thought that someone who sees me at a university fund-raiser chatting about endowments would not recognize me in sweats, shrieking at my children for some frustrating infraction.

Rusty treated a lot of people very well for a long time, and then he killed his wife. If anyone knew what social and genetic factors led him to that, we could probably prevent murder from now on. But I believe that he wasn't a man who plotted an evil deed and gleefully carried it out. I believe the noise in his head got too loud, and he felt completely overwhelmed and out of control, and then he took his wife's life and broke his own heart.

So now we have a mancala board he painted, and I am proud to own it, and also a little sad. Had many things gone differently, Rusty might be painting just for pleasure and taking his canvases and game boards to craft fairs, sitting in the sun and enjoying watching people admire his work. Instead, he lives in the ultimate indoors. He can only read that someone likes his work and perhaps hope that someone remembers that a murderer is a man first. No matter how unforgivable that one act, he also put some good into the world.

arizona's wild women

8 My favorite board game came at Christmas a few years ago: "Wild Women of the West Ride the Trail of Truth." Using little horses for game pieces, the game poses lots of questions on cards, with salty quotes from very self-actualized frontier females.

Sharlot Hall, combing her hair and in a more scholarly pose.

My own collection of literature incorporating pioneer women's journal entries includes some characters of remarkable grit and grace. A decade ago, a book called *Women Who Run with the Wolves* made a splash. Since then, I've realized there are no new ideas, just new ways of presenting them — all art comes out of the same color wheel. Untamed women have been with us always.

I'm not talking professional dilettantes or party girls. I'm talking about the woman in whom a spark of something burns a bit brighter, who maintains a perfectly circumspect life vibrant with the expectancy of something electric about to happen.

Arizona makes a good place for the wild nature of women to flourish, with its mountains to hike and stretches of interstate to speed. One of our foremothers was Sharlot Mabridth Hall.

Coming to Prescott in 1882, just as she turned 12, she was already recording the pulse of the new people and places in her journal, and she became a hearty celebrator of Arizona. At her namesake museum in Prescott, you can see pictures of her hunting, on touring cars in Arizona's remotest corners, and gowned for elegant affairs of state. The most striking photo captures a surprisingly intimate image of her combing her long curtain of wavy hair. But what made Sharlot endure is that she not only experienced many things, she then felt they weren't complete until she wrote about them.

One of the most moving accounts of Territorial Arizona life was her report of a young cavalry captain's wife who'd heard about a newborn baby's death. The young bride took her wedding dress and a new music box to the grieving mother, to make a shroud and a casket. Sharlot was able to immerse herself in subjects, yet hold herself free to explore and experiment.

It's that dual character that to me defines wildness in women: able to function in everyday affairs with efficiency and still indulge the burning impulse to range, to immerse in experiences and interaction.

Sharlot's life was not without sorrow. She and her mother bore the brunt of her father's narrow mind, and she determined never to be "wife," subjugated to a husband's whim. The great love of her life died, never to be truly hers. But she persevered to become Arizona's second Territorial historian, the first woman to hold a salaried position in the Territory's government. Her eloquence and research earned accolades and respect. Representing the state of Arizona during the festivities for President Coolidge's 1925 inauguration, Sharlot wore a remarkable mesh gown woven of Arizona copper. I've always wanted to be Sharlot Hall.

Fortunately, even today's tamer West leaves room for wild spirits to flourish. One I know is Sinclair Browning, who has gathered two adoring reading publics: one for her mysteries and one for her books on spiritual discoveries. With her tumble of hair and exotic ethnic jewelry, she is Jane Fonda without the pretensions. An Arizona woman, Sinclair wrote her first book about Aravaipa Canyon and sets her mystery series in a loose version of Marana. Married to Federal Judge William Browning in Tucson, she is both thoroughly untamable and joyously immersed in their ranch and family.

Another is Elise Wilson, who works as a photographer for KTVK-TV at its northern Arizona news bureau in Flagstaff. Even though her father is an institution at a Los Angeles station's anchor desk, Elise moved here to Arizona and began working a minimum-wage microwave operator's job — a dirty, grueling behind-the-scenes position that is often easiest to blame for anything anywhere. She shoulders through fire camps in dirty protective gear and wears strappy sandals going out. She loves riding her husband's Harley and still weeps when she describes falling in love with him. Wildness is that ability to throw oneself full-throttle into the physical realm and still hold a deep awareness of the unseen.

And Cynthia Billings, who rafted the Colorado River as a crew member and did exuberant cartwheels with her tsunami of multi-colored hair streaming behind her. She scrubbed the Dutch oven and hauled the boat to tie off onshore, but still wore long skirts preparing dinner. Wild women don't take the middle ground; they straddle the extremes.

I imagine wild women are often exhausted. There aren't enough hours to dance every dance, meet every member of one's tribe, and still build an impressive résumé without sacrificing time to rest. But that's the price of passage on the journey worth taking to wild women.

Wild women don't bother carrying membership cards, and they never identify themselves as such. You will notice them perhaps despite their conventional business apparel or the minivans they drive. The crackling energy seeps through undaunted.

Sharlot Hall summed this up in her usual gorgeous way in a letter to Matthew Riordan, of the Flagstaff pioneer family:

"I am so glad, so glad, so glad that God let me be an outdoor woman and love the big things. I couldn't be a tame housecat woman and spend big sunny, glorious days giving card parties and planning dresses. I'm not unwomanly — don't you dare to think so — but God made women to joy in his great, clean, beautiful world — and I thank Him that he lets me see some of it not through a windowpane."

world under glass

9 It looks like a project using Legos and Tupperware gone out of control. As you follow the winding highway north of Tucson to the town of Oracle and Biosphere II, you feel steeped in nature, yet as you walk down the path toward the Biosphere's buildings, nothing could look less natural. As the tour guide explains, 50 tons of stainless steel, 77,000 steel struts, and thousands of sheets of glass form this glittering spread. Cathedral-like space, domes, and turrets spread out like a medieval fiefdom envisioned by a space-age architect.

Biosphere II sets a rain forest in the foothills of the Catalina Mountains.

49

Biosphere II started as a billionaire's science project back in the 1980s, when Edward P. Bass dreamed of creating an experimental closed system where varieties of life, including human, could thrive sealed off from the outside world. Some said the experiment primarily looked ahead to future space stations. During construction, reporters were occasionally invited out to the site to deliver progress reports. At the time, it was easy to poke mild fun at the jumpsuited workers who spoke urgently into their hand-held radios if anyone strayed off the path or appeared to not be paying attention. One reporter remarked sotto voce that what truly got them going was if you appeared to be munching something as you strolled through the greenhouse, where crops were being cultivated to sustain the "Bionauts" during their upcoming mission — living for two years in a sealed, hopefully self-sufficient world.

In 1991, eight Bionauts entered Biosphere II for what must have been the longest two years of their lives.

Once the doors opened, and the eight were released back out onto Biosphere I (Earth), the Biosphere seemed to undergo post-partum depression. The ultimate lab without the ultimate quest dropped from public view. But Columbia University took over the campus, and now some 1,000 people per week tour this giant creation.

If NASA and Disney were to collaborate on a theme park, it would look like this. Gift shops geared to different areas of the Biosphere pop up as you follow the curving path. Strategically spaced, two restaurants anticipate your hunger pangs. And yet the tour guide's intriguing narrative makes me wish a press corps were present again, so fascinating and potentially momentous are the experiments underway.

For your admission fee, you get a tour of the outside of Biosphere II, with the most knowledgeable speaker I have ever encountered at any scientific facility, from the Palo Verde Nuclear Generating Station to the Titan Missile Museum. (I've gone out on a limb here — I hope all the guides are as good.) From outside the windows, you are introduced to the enclosed worlds of rain forest, desert, savanna, marsh, and ocean.

You hear, of course, about what Mr. Bass bought with some $400 million: the 250-acre property now hosting both undergraduate and graduate students from Columbia University, with classes in various sciences taught by full professors (they get to live in darling little barrio-colored lodges).

The original premise of Biosphere II — a closed universe — remains. The variation on the theme is that now elements such as humidity, temperature, and air mix can be deliberately altered. Why would one do that? For one reason, to recreate the conditions on Earth during different ages. Then, based on data and atmospheric and climatic trends, future conditions can be created. This system is complex and delicate: On the inside tour, we were warned to turn off cell phones and pagers, since the signal of one ringing has cued an instant rainstorm.

This inside tour, called "Under the Glass," which made me feel like an oyster, lets you do more than ogle: You walk where the Bionauts tread. Children may be crushed to learn that the three spirited monkeys who kept company with the eight crew members are gone: They fought, and keeping them in the closed system would make it harder to change living conditions for plants without worrying about affecting their well-being. But insects and sea creatures remain.

Yes, sea creatures. Perhaps Biosphere II's most arresting aspect is the ocean: a 25-foot deep reservoir of salt water descended from the Pacific Ocean, with all the same microbes and plant life. A lung-type arrangement sends rhythmic "waves," which can be set from 3 inches to 3 feet high, to keep the water moving and faithfully replicate marine conditions. There used to be quite a bit more beach on one end, the guide dryly explained, but setting the waves at 3 feet once swept much of the beach to the bottom of the tank. The guide also described the four men and four women diving off the cliff into the deep water; an Elvis movie image in a sci-fi setting.

It's odd to stand looking out at the dry, desert hills around Oracle while breathing in the heavy humid air of the "rain forest," surrounded by banana trees and a lush canopy of jungle growth. Odd also to walk underground through the tunnel that parallels the "ocean," and try to remember you're in Arizona.

While the pricey plush toys and bright playsets in the gift shops may initially beguile younger tourists, the biosphere complex also treats them to tremendous exhibits. The captivating underwater display charms the most reluctant child with a small "beach" to play on, clown fish in natural-looking aquariums, and an experiment with visualizing shells. Even a walk through the greenhouses is constructed to be interesting to children. Bright signs, invitations to observe photosynthesis, and hands-on displays are impressive.

The level of research being carried on also impressed me. It might be tempting to write off Biosphere II as an anomaly in the desert, an eccentric's bubble of dreams that has outlived its usefulness. But listening to explanations of research being conducted slams home that what began as something for space research could ultimately save Biosphere I from human damage. Coral reef research is yielding information that applies to our oceans, and many plant projects are bearing scientific fruit.

One in particular stayed with me. Global warming and fossil fuels contaminating the environment pose an increasing problem, and our guide mentioned that the "rainforest" section has indicated that there is a limit to how much carbon dioxide those plants can convert to oxygen. That's bad. A grove of cottonwood trees, however, has been shown to absorb twice as much carbon dioxide as the rainforest. That's good. Walking up to lunch, I was wondering if Mr. Bass's dream, after providing fodder for irreverent observers in the past, may end up providing a key we vitally need to survive. I find myself hoping, for the sake of dreamers everywhere willing to pursue their ideas, that Mr. Bass has the last laugh. His willingness to pursue scientific truths may provide us all with a precious, priceless breath of fresh air.

MARCH

the secret tucson

10

Any traveler knows that guidebooks give lots of good information, but that to get below the surface, it's best to talk to a native. Having been born in Tucson means I can share some of the places you wouldn't necessarily know about otherwise.

Places like the El Encanto neighborhood, off Broadway Boulevard and Country Club Road, where leading families built homes, each distinct from its neighbor. Beside the sprawling haciendas and Territorial estates you might expect, you'll also see architectural details like widow's

The Farmer John Meats mural adds distinction along Flowing Wells Road.

walks and columns deserving of southern plantations. In spring, we used to slowly drive the curving streets to admire the gardens and rapturously inhale the alluring scent of orange blossoms.

Sabino Canyon shows up in most guidebooks, but know that you'll have to park your car at the visitors center, leaving you the options of hoofing it into the canyon or taking the shuttle tram. If you decide to run the meandering road to the top, it's a better-than-7-mile round trip along flowing Sabino Creek. In the winter, expect some icy wading where the creek water from Mount Lemmon's snowmelt surges across the road. In the summer, you will sweat the sweat of champions even under the shady canopy of streamside trees. If you are lucky, you will hear the downward trill of a canyon wren, which sounds like the tiny bird is tumbling backward off its hidden perch.

If you don't feel right without seeing a monument or statue, Tucson's downtown delivers two unique ones. A county park, the Garden of Gethsemane lies practically under Interstate 10 at the Broadway exit. Just west of the underpass, you find Felix Lucero's fulfillment of a promise to God. Lucero vowed that if he came home from the trenches of World War I, he would create art glorifying Jesus. (In this improbable location, it seems like finding some original folios of Shakespeare tucked under the corner of a museum's area rug.) You can see Mary and Joseph sculpted life-size, virtually pull up a chair to the Last Supper to look around at the disciples' faces, and gaze up at the crucified Christ. This is inspirational folk art at its finest.

Another shrine, with more impromptu origins, is *El Tiradito*, the "Little Outcast's" wishing shrine, said to be the only such site to glorify a sinner buried in unhallowed ground. Go south on Main from Broadway to Cushing and you find the wrought iron stand with perpetual candles, where wishers leave mementos like flowers and ribbons. The legend is that a lovers' triangle, possibly involving a mother-in-law, resulted in the shooting of Juan Olivera in about 1880. People come to offer petitions, both general and specific, for sinners.

Go back to Broadway and head east until Country Club, then keep an eye out for what appears to be a church tower to the north. It isn't, really — my befuddled parents circled the area as newcomers, trying to find the cathedral they assumed was in there somewhere. It is a water tower built as a companion piece to the gorgeous El Conquistador Hotel, which was demolished to make room for El Con Shopping Center across the street. I don't believe we would let that demolition happen today, but the city was tipsy on progress and still salted with enough old buildings to be cavalier.

Now old buildings that survived the boom of the 1960s are guarded like sultans' wives. Downtown offers walking tours of homes that incorporated part of the original presidio wall, dating to when Tucson was belonged to New Spain. Long before Tucson was part of the Gadsden Purchase in 1854, some residents in 1777 heard that another struggling group of colonists was fighting to gain a foothold in the New World and sent 459 pesos to help the patriots back east.

On North Swan Road, you have Ted DeGrazia's studio, the Gallery of the Sun, with the artist's final resting place on the grounds. His whimsically decorated chapel, gallery, and outbuildings feel as if he could have just stepped out for a beer. He built the adobe rooms by hand and pulled together found objects — tin cans, tobacco packages, and paint to decorate them. His paintings hang throughout.

So many rich fabrics share the quilt of Tucson culture, it's hard to pick favorite pieces. It is steeped deep in the local tea. One place locals proudly bring visitors to is Austin's Ice Cream Parlor ("since 1959"). Austin's is wonderful because of its unabashed dedication to flavor over fat reduction. In this time of carb-gram awareness, Austin's is like a very large woman wearing a wild tropical print instead of trying to look slimmer in black, celebrating the abundance instead of apologizing for it. The ice cream, so creamy it almost glimmers as if lit from within, is worth every one of the 16 grams of fat.

At the corner of Grant Road and Interstate 10, the Farmer John

Meats processing plant stands out for its elaborate mural of cattle scenes. Drive around the back, heading north. Once you are on Flowing Wells Road, turn south again and drive straight toward the realistic bull facing you, dust forever boiling up from his pounding hooves. Continue toward him, making any noises you feel appropriate, and drive into the dirt until your nerve fails you. Please know your limits so the painting may be preserved for others to enjoy. My family called this "charging the bull" and made it a favorite pursuit ever since my father created it, one Sunday afternoon drive, for four wildly excited children and one apprehensive wife.

One thing I would never do is pick a single Mexican restaurant to recommend as the best — it's too subjective. When my brother visits from California, he heads for Casa Molina, with its round room and potent margaritas. My mother likes the El Charro on the east side, with a bright private patio. I am fond of El Torerro in South Tucson, with the wall-mounted fish and luscious cheese tacos.

I will recommend what I think is the best parking spot. While "A" Mountain and the north end of Swan Road have their fans, Gates Pass at the west end of Speedway Boulevard offers an unparalleled view of the Saguaro National Park from its mountain perch. Watch the sunset. Walk to one of the ramadas and harmonize if you like.

Leonard Cohen wrote, "Everyone who wanted you, found what he will always want again." So it is with Tucson.

how green was my valley

11 When I was 12, my friend Jean moved to a new home in the Tucson foothills. The day my friends and I went over for the first time, Chris took one look at the living room's expanse of green carpet framed by white arches and said, "It looks like Green Valley!"

The Spanish style's tile roofs, arches, and tile floors influence Green Valley buildings.

Ten years later, when I arrived in Green Valley for my first job as a cub reporter, I saw the East Valley Community Center and understood what she meant.

I was as new and shiny as any raw recruit, bursting with good intentions and misconceptions. The residents numbered in the teen-thousands, and for the first few weeks, all looked alike to me, as new classmates do when you change schools. The first day on the job, I type-set golf and bridge scores for the newspaper and thought I understood the pulse of community life. I could not have been more wrong.

Their leisure activities no more define Green Valley residents than a child is defined by a scooter or a television. They may spend time this way, but the living is a much broader and more complicated thing.

Having been given a front row seat to a retirement community, I now bristle when I hear someone refer to them as "elephant graveyards" or dismiss them as a bunch of snippy retirees who can't handle the real world any longer. I see a retirement community more like a college dorm, where people gather with their kind. Every other age seeks out its own: from playgrounds at parks where you find an instant friend because she's on the swing next to you, to suburbs, where if you are lucky, the woman across the street becomes your partner in home happy hour, watching your children play. Green Valley attracted people who didn't want to shovel snow any longer, who wanted plenty of social and civic involve-ment, and who looked for big clean spaces to pursue their interests. Like any place, some residents were more social than others. I met them most, of course.

Working at the *Green Valley News* was a little like having hundreds of well-meaning parents and grandparents. When I haphazardly described someone as "beautific," a subscriber walked into the office the next day, with the article clipped and edited in red, and gently explained the connection to "beatitude," not "beautiful." More personally, when I was seen having lunch with a married physician, my editor got two phone calls informing him of my whereabouts before I returned to the office. It takes a village to raise a reporter.

When I drive through Green Valley, the scenery triggers stories that unfolded there. Driving past the modern architecture of Community Center West (West Center and East Center were like West and East Egg in Fitzgerald's mythical Hamptons — everyone who needed to, understood the terms), I remember a holiday lunch where each table had a centerpiece of painstakingly miniature gifts, wrapped and tied in the tiniest of ribbons. At first it broke my heart than anyone had taken hours of life working on something so fleeting. Then I began to understand the pleasure lies in the creating — a lesson that would be borne out again at craft shows and gourmet restaurants the rest of my life.

Seeing East Center recalls the community council meetings where I first grasped the value of retirement communities. In a major city, too many of these people would have been shoved aside by the younger elk coming up. But here, Perc Williams and Walter McKinley and Hans Hoel and the rest grappled with the financial and social issues that confront a group of any size. I saw how churches stepped in to quietly locate and help the lonely, the alcoholic, and the poor. And while it was rumored Green Valley banks swelled by millions the day Social Security checks were mailed, I saw fixed incomes evidenced in the careful, modest purchases of someone behind me in line at the grocery store. The county building reminds me of going every Monday morning to see what the police blotter contained, talking to the deputy no woman had ever had reason to dislike, and learning that even small towns of older residents had heartbreak and conflict and greed and sorrow.

It was at the main grocery store I learned the hard lesson of what not to say when someone recognizes you. The clerk who took my check scrutinized me and said, "Oh, I know you. I read your work in the paper."

Pleased and flustered, I said, "Do you like it?"

"No," she said flatly. "I don't."

But most people I interviewed were kinder teachers. I still think of Rosalind Herrick, who I met when I did a feature on her rosemaling work, saying that there is nothing so permanent as a temporary fixture. I remember the Valley National Bank president giving me her business philosophy: "Attitude, like rain, comes from above."

I was privileged to attend the Rotary meetings and women's club luncheons that attracted wonderful speakers, from Barry Goldwater to Will Rogers Jr. I remember my delight sitting at Marjel DeLauer's table while her friend, actress Jane Russell, cleared our lunch dishes. (It was Marjel, slim in her jeans and coifed hair, who also told me, "Act delighted to see a man, but always let him know how happy you are even when he's not there. It makes him want to be there.")

So many people in Green Valley had learned the pleasure of taking time for others. When I wrote of a poem my grandma used to recite, I mourned that I couldn't remember what came after "It was midnight on the ocean, not a streetcar was in sight." No fewer than 12 readers found stamps and wrote out the rest of the rhyme. I still wish I had a sociologist to explain why no two versions were the same.

I sat in living rooms and on patios with views of the golf course and listened to soft voices describe the fading blue numbers inked on wrists of their stunned and shocked childhood selves at the prison camps of Germany and Poland. I watched women quilting in a church activity center and heard the quiet talk of how hard it was for people of their generation to accept charity and how the Depression had shaped them. Sometimes, recollections of a telegram received during wartime still quivered an upper lip and brought understanding touches from others. People had seen their children die, lost fortunes, and battled depression. But like Bill Wight, the mildly avuncular, pipe-smoking columnist who sat at the desk next to me, they demonstrated that the better part of life is just showing up.

Even when I've forgotten the names, the lessons have endured. The woman who had been a girl during the Blitz in London described in modulated tones her mother's china cabinet, full of delicate dishes, suddenly blasted to smithereens by a German bomb: "So use your good things — don't keep them put away waiting for a special occasion."

The man who reflected on his life as a political figure and said mildly that opponents and critics weren't angry as much as afraid.

And I remember interviewing a candidate running for Fire Board who was so appealing in his gentility that I realized being over 60 wasn't the opposite of being attractive.

I met couples who had been high school sweethearts and found one another again after their respective and well-loved spouses had died. I attended my first funeral of a friend who died of breast cancer and saw how people who have endured sorrow develop the ability to feel grief without thinking it will kill them.

I left Green Valley almost four years to the day after I first drove there past the exits I came to know by heart: Sahuarita, the mine roads, San Xavier. I was moving to a long-coveted job in television news in Tucson, but I think even at the time I knew what I was giving up. It was like being on the temple steps, listening to the elders, absorbing what collective centuries had to offer. It was like a university education, taught by the masters. I hope if in some future time a young reporter comes to do a feature story on my collection of Arizona coffee mugs, I am able to pass on some of what Green Valley gave to me.

being a brick

12 Pulling over to read a historical marker at the side of the road used to feel like getting my teeth cleaned — this will be good for me, but unpleasant. As an adult, I'm glad my father insisted on pausing to collect what he calls "the bright bits of information stored in the crow's nest of my mind." And I have discovered another kind of historical marker, put up without state approval or legislative statute.

These are the commemorative bricks that pave patios and monuments around the state. Usually sold as fundraisers for some good cause, they are the common person's anthem to what is held dear, a public patchwork quilt of sentimental favorites. Strolling around a collection of inscriptions like this reminds me of window shopping for memories. It's almost like reading single sentences from a hundred different diaries.

A ceremonial brick is a hybrid between legal graffiti and a tombstone for the living. One of my favorite monument quotations is on the Northern Arizona University campus in Flagstaff. Across from the Old Main building is a quote from a venerable and valuable man, J. Lawrence Walkup, who was NAU's president during the 1950s and 60s. It reads:

"To become educated is to become more human."

Significant that he didn't say "is to become superior to the masses,"

Bricks at Flagstaff's veterans' memorial, top, and in Winslow send perpetual messages.

or "is to increase your earning power," but "is to become more human."

So it's nice to be able to express our own humanity nearby. The university erected its Centennial Clock a few years ago, with many NAU alumni and families pitching in with personalized bricks. Spread out under your feet stretches a time capsule you don't have to wait to open. Our family went for the jumbo model brick, in order to outline my father's lifelong association with what was Arizona State College when he learned to ski down the slope by the Old Main building: "Here, Larry Schnebly saw his father teach, met and courted Lee, showed compassion and humor as housing director . . . played with his children and grandchildren." He didn't have to die for us to salute some of his contributions in stone.

Farther east along Interstate 40 In Winslow, my mother and her brother share their tribute to the town where they grew up (I guess bricks run in my blood). They planted theirs on the street corner of "standin' on" fame that has become a photo op for tourists since the Eagles song, "Take It Easy," came out in the 1970s. Long before its immortalization in rock music, brother and sister walked around that corner on their way downtown for sodas and movies. In fact, both worked on different points of "The Corner" — my mother as a waitress on the breakfast shift of the Grand Café, and Uncle Paul cleaning up after hours in what is now the Route 66, but was a jewelry store back then.

"We got our starts here, and left our hearts here," their brick reads.

A brick I bought for a Vietnam veteran's memorial in the Flagstaff cemetery says: "Randall. For friends."

It is a lasting toast to a photographer I worked with who brought Vietnam home and gave me insights I will never forget. One early morning on a run in Flagstaff, I remembered I'd paid for the brick and went to find it. I was unprepared for the emotional power of all those words chiseled in cement. The paving was a mute amalgam of strangers' loves and regrets, no less powerful in their anonymity.

The one that struck the deepest was: "Dad — I taught John to fish."

Had they used to fish together? Did he always think of his father when he took his son fishing? Others were messages of holidays never to be celebrated, a daughter facing the walk down the aisle with a memory instead of a dad. Here the bricks remind us that official casualty counts are individual lives, each with widening circles of those who love them.

(One of the best bricks I ever saw admittedly was not in Arizona: After the 1989 San Francisco earthquake, John Otte wrote for a Golden Gate restoration: "It is the mettle of the people that makes the gate golden.")

At the other extreme, my brother Lindsay opted for post-modern dispassion when he ordered his University of Arizona alumni brick from his surfside home in California. "It sure is hot here," was his message to all and sundry.

In the metropolitan Phoenix area, I have walked through Paradise Valley Mall, entertained by the sentiments people chose to share with us, the audience of strangers: little nicknames, declarations of love (are those couples still together?), birthday wishes. While for me, they may be no more than diverting captions between steps, each one meant enough to someone that they wanted to tell the world.

Wise hospitals capitalize on this desire to leave one's mark in public places with Tree of Life sculptures. My parents have purchased for each grandchild a "leaf" on the Tree of Life at Good Samaritan Hospital in Phoenix. This "tree" grows more rapidly than most living ones, as grateful family members tell the world about their new addition.

A permanent announcement like this is the average citizen's equivalent of a marble statue in the courthouse square, a permanent, public love letter. It's carving initials in a sanctioned tree, a community of our tributes. While a little less eye-catching than an 8-foot bronze general on a horse, the strength lies in the weight of our combined intentions: to honor, to share.

To remember.

interstate 17, interpreted

13 Happiness is driving Interstate 17 from Phoenix to Flagstaff. I know no finer feeling than starting that two-hour, 5,000-foot roadside tour of Arizona. When I reported news from Flagstaff for Phoenix station KTVK and my husband worked for the same station in Phoenix, I drove that stretch more than 200 times in two years, Friday evenings and Monday mornings. Discoveries happened like the weeds that grew up between the two lanes of asphalt. I never would truly have grasped how far north and south the sun moves as seasons change — from having it in my eyes to behind my head. And from leaving in chilly pitch black in December, arriving in an icy Flagstaff around sunup, to having the sun beat me to the punch even as I crept out before 5 A.M. in June. I learned you can make a big muffin last all the way to Badger Springs, if you eat slowly enough, and how long you can go once the "low fuel" light comes on. But most of all, I learned the exits.

Each green highway sign was a bead on the string of my trek, many with their own stories. I have yet to find the right party, but I remain sure that somewhere exists a group that would love to hear the exits recited in order, sort of like naming the state capitals. So until I find them, I recite them for myself, every so often, seeing in my mind's eye the

The San Francisco Peaks loom on Verde Valley's north horizon.

surroundings of the exit signs. Heading north from Phoenix, they are:

Deer Valley
Pinnacle Peak
Happy Valley
Carefree Highway
Pioneer
Anthem (was Desert Hills)

I regret the change in signage there, because it once seemed to say that Carefree Pioneers, Happy to leave the Valley, Deserted the Hills . . . and shortly went on to Table the Mesa. (Table Mesa being one leg of the Spanish-English redundancy tripod of Arizona place names, along with Picacho Peak and the Rillito River.) Pioneer, or Pioneer Arizona Living History Museum, harbors one of my favorite buildings in the state, the old church. I've been photographing that since high school.

New River
Table Mesa
Rock Springs

One of my brothers began referring to the Rock Springs Café as the "Dollar Steakhouse," after years of my singing its economic and epicurean praises. Some folks exalt the pies . . . I like the canned vegetables and butter packets, alongside what I recall as rhapsodically good steak.

Mud Springs
Black Canyon City

On this steep climb up the Bradshaw Mountain grade, let us give thanks for slower drivers who stay right and say a prayer for the reckless who endanger us all.

Bumble Bee
Crown King

Bloody Basin
Badger Springs
My cousin Mel, who became a low-country transplant and brought her southern fiancé out west to meet the folks, told me Bud had been astonished at the challenging way Arizona names sites. No Magnolia Road and Dogwood Place for us: Bloody Basin, Dead Horse State Park, Devil Dog Road. "No wonder y'all are so . . . direct," Bud said.

Cordes Junction
Prescott
As a youngster, I pointed out how charming it was that the piñon pine and juniper trees that define the Mogollon Rim's look begin in a cluster right at the Cordes exit. My father said mildly that probably the state highway department had played a big part in that, which then seemed blatantly obvious. But I still like those high-country ambassadors at Milepost 168.

Dugas-Orme
Cherry Road
If you watch the rocky cuts the freeway passes through, there will be two right here that are appropriately cherry-colored — naturally.

Camp Verde
When you begin pulling around the bends that lead into the Verde Valley, expect your first distant view of Flagstaff's San Francisco Peaks. It used to come just after a sign advertising Woody's Exxon, but that sign is now gone. Still those magnificent volcanic sentries of the north stand stalwart and constant. I always take a deep breath and feel like I'm home.

General Crook Trail
Middle Verde
Montezuma

Many times making this run, I stopped at the Texaco Starmart at this exit. The man who worked the morning shift got used to me and always merrily offered me a doughnut that I always refused. Once when I stood in line, the tourist in front of me had an unusual last name that the clerk noticed, and it turned out the two had grown up a few streets apart in a small Minnesota town. We were delighted, every one of us.

McGuireville-Cornville

If you've never shot pool at the McGuireville Tavern on a weekday afternoon, you haven't experienced all Arizona has to offer.

Sedona
Stoneman Lake

During winter snows, here is where you either need chains going north or you're out of the worst driving heading south. It's now 35 minutes to Flagstaff.

Fox Ranch (was Woods Canyon)

While I regard the Fox family with as much respect as Riordans and Babbitts for their contributions to northern Arizona, when this sign changed, I missed the thematic trio of stone, wood, and rock exit names.

Rocky Park
Schnebly Hill Road

I've never found anyone who can explain this, but there is an inordinate number of snags around here. The stark spare shapes of these still-standing dead trees abound on both sides of the road. Does the geography draw fatal lightning strikes to the trees of this area? Also, here you'll catch your next look of the Peaks.

Munds Park

Just like Parks on Interstate 40 west of Flagstaff, this place is a storm magnet. I have crept, rigid, across sheets of ice on this road, isolated by blowing snow and sobered by the tracks that swerved off the road to disabled vehicles, only to find clear skies a few miles north.

Willard Springs
Newman Park
Kelly Canyon
Mountainaire
My one trip to traffic school came courtesy of the patrol officer who quite rightly nabbed me as I sailed with more speed than caution through this stretch.

Flagstaff Airport
The airport's desegregation in the early 1950s occurred because my father, NAU student Mugnii Danmoli from Africa, and Sam Van Dyck, a football player from Winslow, were refused service at the coffee shop one Sunday night. Shocked, my father told Wilson Riles, who did a jazz show as "Dr. Rhythm" on KGPH in Flagstaff. Riles went to the City Council to point out that if an African dignitary were to be refused service at the gateway to the Grand Canyon, it could reflect poorly on Flagstaff worldwide. The airport was desegregated.

Lake Mary
Flagstaff
Right on the edge of town, the J.W. Powell Boulevard overpass always makes me wonder if it's named after the Colorado River explorer, gutsy, one-armed John Wesley Powell. Yes, I could ask. But my natural pessimism makes me afraid I wouldn't like the answer. The Peaks rise benevolently ahead.

You have arrived.

at sunrise rejoicing

14

Easter in Arizona.

What rich and varied arrangements of the one theme we play. Christ is risen; alleluia.

At the Grand Canyon, pilgrims begin gathering before 6 A.M., huddled in jackets, ducking their chins into scarves, wishing for coffee. They stand facing the chasm blurred by darkness, and as the choir sings of the Risen Son, the rising sun touches, awakens the spires and buttresses, valleys and edges. Dawn colors of coral, thin yellow, and deep violet emerge. "How Great Thou Art" sung next to the Grand Canyon at an Easter sunrise service leaves a permanent memory of awe, a sharp, almost piercing awareness of the inextricable link between God's majesty and people's place here on Earth.

Traditionally in Tucson, mariachis strum "De Colores" as the colors of morning creep up the eastern slope of "A" Mountain. The huge stark wooden cross has been carried haltingly up the slope by strong tired men. Now ribbons and flowers flutter from it in the first breeze of day. Many people here are of Hispanic descent: Older women, who can feel the sacrifice of letting one's son die, give fervent thanks for Christ's resurrection and for their many children and grandchildren, sometimes

The South Rim of the Grand Canyon displays one of its infinite appearances.

73

holding the soft pliant hand of a beloved toddler. The priest points out how the sun touches faces, transforms the world with light, ". . . like the Son. He touches us, and we are illumined."

Easter is a Christian holiday, but also universal with its links to the cycle of life and diverse traditions. The only event on the church calendar linked to the moon, it moves because the Jewish Passover is not a fixed date on our modern calendar. Not that Easter is a Jewish holiday, but it marks in Christian history events that pivoted on Jewish tradition. The Last Supper, Jesus celebrating his final Passover, triggered what led to the Crucifixion. Passover commemorates the early Jews, ready to leave slavery in Egypt, saving their firstborn sons by sprinkling sacrificial lamb's blood on their doorposts. *Pascua Dominica* means "Sunday of the Lamb" in Latin. Which brings us to another Arizona culture: the tribes of southern Arizona.

When Father Kino came to the Tohono O'odham people in the 1700s, he had to present Catholicism in a context that made sense to their culture. Even today, Mission San Xavier del Bac differs vastly from a Catholic church in downtown Phoenix: The festivals at San Xavier, humming with the merry, polka-like music some call chicken-scratch, pulse with vibrancy and color. Statues of saints bear offerings from the faithful and prints of pilgrims' kisses. Like a grandparent with a copious lap, the church has room for all.

Yaqui Indians fleeing persecution in Mexico settled near Tucson when they received about 40 acres as a homesite. The Yaqui Pascua Village is named to commemorate this gift given on Easter Sunday in 1921. Father Dan McLaughlin, S.P., said the congregation of about 4,000 Yaquis use the Latin term Pascua for both Easter and Passover.

The Yaqui celebration of Easter shows how inclusive the holiday is. The deer dancers, cantoras (singers), and coyote dancers all figure into the elaborate, intense celebration of Easter.

Father McLaughlin said two early Spanish missionaries faced reaching some 30,000 Yaquis and relied on the tribe to spread the teachings of

Christ among themselves. So established Yaqui lore and customs were drawn in from the beginning. Most observances of Easter include a penance, or reconciliation, before Easter Sunday. But only the Yaquis have the ceremony of lashing, and masked dancers representing the gathering forces of evil crawling through the trees hunting for Christ. It escalates to a clash between the forces of good and evil on Saturday — an orchestrated mayhem of violence. What contrast between that and the stately procession and groomed lilies of an Episcopal High Mass!

And the incorporation of other cultures and symbols goes farther back. The linguistic roots of the word "Easter" are ancient Anglo-Saxon, for Eastre, the Nordic goddess of the dawn. The lighting of the Pascual candle with New Fire and blessing of the Holy Water harken back to pagan festivals of spring, with new fire and water. Even the Easter symbols of egg and bunny are obvious holdovers from the fertility celebrations of ancient springtimes.

Father Richard Milligan at St. Luke's in north Phoenix advised the congregation one Palm Sunday that the ranks would swell on Easter with non-season ticket holders, and urged people to be hospitable to the newcomers. People seem to need to celebrate Easter in church more than other feast days.

"People who have no formal faith at all come to church on Easter Sunday," said Father Tim Davern. "Most cultures have some sort of new life festival." Maybe it's innate in humankind to want to applaud springtime, to glory in dew and dawn as new water and new light.

Whether at a small but consistent gathering of pilgrims at Morris Udall Park in Tucson or at a packed house at one of the evangelical pageants, we are touched by sunrise services, where light bursts physically as well as spiritually upon the darkened world. I love knowing Easter, with its central truth, weaves and decorates with contributions from around the globe.

"Holy" wars — the most horrible oxymoron I know — are fought, and much blood is spilled over religious differences. But acceptance exists in Easter, named for a pagan fertility rite and unfolding from Jewish Passover, bringing the symbols of blood and lamb. It is now celebrated in Arizona with a melding of Jesuit teachings brought across the sea in the 1600s and told to a tribe using their own story of the deer dancer.

So many peoples have contributed to the celebration of Easter. As new tender green appears in the desert, as light comes kindly at an earlier hour, it seems right to gather and renew our belief. Being able to see and feel life returning makes it easier to feel the things we cannot see. And say "alleluia!"

a grand lady's gift

15 You may never design buildings, but you can have something in common with Frank Lloyd Wright when you enjoy a cocktail at Tucson's Arizona Inn lounge.

Wright apparently appreciated the airy old room with its domed skylight; I don't know if it was the deep-cushioned couches grouped for conversation, the stately grand piano, or the gleaming mahogany bar, but the fact that the famous architect resonated to this obscure, dignified hideaway doesn't surprise. It always seems like where Hemingway

Hacienda architecture helps define the Arizona Inn.

77

would have become a regular had he been in Tucson. Writers, architects — who wouldn't want to settle in with a libation of choice and wax eloquent?

It's not recorded what Wright thought of the Arizona Inn library, but the high-ceilinged room with its ox-sized fireplace and shadowed corners beguiles most everyone. With afternoon tea, the 30-foot pine tree wafting Christmas through the air during the holiday season, and the elegantly worn high-backed chairs, the library is the set for many a whispered conversation, momentous meeting, and stately reception. Patty Doar, granddaughter of the inn's founder, Isabella Greenway, said she sees more young people drawn to the inn, perhaps for a glimpse of graciousness they've never known.

"Recently, I saw a young man bring his girlfriend here, and while he showed her library, I eavesdropped shamelessly," she confessed. "He said, 'This room makes you feel like . . . you could even write a letter!'"

The Arizona Inn does seem to soothe a nostalgic yearning for what we never had; it's the family mansion we wish our grandparents had built with railroad money and filled with heirlooms. Just northeast of the University of Arizona, it is a sanctuary unto itself. It is breakfast as elegant as anyone else's dinner; fat brown birds feasting off crumbs as you unwind on the patio while watching a thunderstorm come in over the mountains. And for some fortunates, it's an annual pilgrimage that began decades ago. Doar said some longtime winter visitors who came as children now bring their own offspring.

Many consider the Arizona Inn the grande dame of the state's hotels; opened in 1930, she is technically a senior citizen. But like her founder, Isabella Greenway, the lady makes aging a graceful art.

The staff of the 86-room hideaway in the center of town honors two priorities: making every visitor extremely comfortable, and keeping Greenway's spirit alive. Which I noticed immediately when I spoke to the manager's secretary about coming by and said I would ask for her at the desk.

"Not at all," she answered. "You relax in the library, and we will come to you."

Had you walked into the Arizona Inn 50 years ago, you would have noticed the Territorial architecture, with thick sunset-colored adobe walls and cobalt blue trim; the lazy invitation of deep green lawns, flowers fairly spilling over their borders along brick paths. You might have peeked into the dining room where lanterns and heavy silver were being arranged for dinner or strolled the white arched lobby where footsteps are muffled in thick carpet. Had you gone past the Har-Tru tennis courts to the pool, you could have seen couples eating lunch on wooden chaises near whimsically painted windows while staff hovered benevolently but alertly nearby.

You might have gone to your room and found fine old linens, a writing desk, a closet large enough for the steamer trunks winter visitors would bring, and a small collection of entertaining books.

You would still find all those things today.

The only difference is that had you walked into the Arizona Inn during the 1950s, Isabella Greenway would probably have been capably attending to something on the property. So elegant a woman that she quite literally caused a traffic jam while touring Paris at the age of 16, the Greenway shown in photographs wears large shady hats and gauzy white dresses. But she was far from merely decorative — Doar remembered her grandmother being the center of activity, looking for fun, and making the least involved feel included.

"She was always curious and interested and had an enormous appetite for whatever was going on," Doar said of the woman who was also Arizona's first congresswoman, serving from 1933 to 1937. "She would never do anything I would consider indecorous, but she was in no way rigid. Nothing could have been more boring to her than having only one kind of people in her life — or her inn."

Greenway began the Arizona Inn with little thought of social status or future profit. She was merely becoming her own customer for piles of furniture. In a characteristically energetic and empathetic act, she had started the Arizona Hut, a furniture factory, after World War I. Servicemen weakened by illness and poison gas came in droves to Arizona and couldn't work strenuous schedules, so she founded the Hut (named after the refuges from the front lines) and let veterans work flexible schedules. But the Crash of '29 brought an end to buyers like Marshal Field and Abercrombie & Fitch. Faced with $22,000 owed to herself as investor, she created a new market: the Arizona Inn.

The inn still houses many Hut originals: dining room tables and chairs, desks and beds in private rooms, and heavy public room pieces. Other antiques came from Greenway's private collection. On a saunter through the inn, 19th-century Audubon prints, relics in the Africa Room from her safari, and antique Spanish Colonial ceramics arrest the eye.

The Arizona Inn has room for all our memories. Doar said one woman told her she liked weddings at the inn so much, she got married there twice!

The staff honors the code of confidentiality so thoroughly that you must confirm through others' memoirs and photographs that the Duke and Duchess of Windsor, Lowell Thomas, and Clark Gable were all guests. So was Eleanor Roosevelt, to whom Greenway was a bridesmaid. Longtime majordomo Maynard Pike remarked once that Mrs. Roosevelt was truly gracious, "but always looked as if she needed a lady's maid to give her a good brushup."

He wouldn't give away, however, what famous African-American singer stayed at the inn, lodging there because Greenway was the only Tucson innkeeper at the time who would "take a colored." (A true lady, Greenway lived out good breeding by valuing people, not ranking them; once when she hired a black worker, she quenched rumblings among the staff by seating him next to her at lunch.)

Service far above and beyond is what endears the inn to people. Mr. Pike recalled that Mr. Room 187 needed a no-salt diet, and for years Pike was in charge of his special menu. File cards of guests' relatives were kept so guests would never repeat a gift. Doar recalled her grandmother's legendary near-obsession with comfort when she was shepherding the construction of the inn.

"She made workmen carry sawhorses and a pillow," she said. "She would lie down where beds were going to be, to see the view out the window." When the pool and porches were being added, Greenway had posts set out so she could follow the sun's progress across the sky and see how far awnings would need to extend to shade guests' eyes.

She also cloistered them; most of the rooms open onto patios with entrances tucked behind tall hedges. But one can only do so much — Doar laughed when describing frantic efforts to keep the arrival of a famous singer a secret, only to have a clearly labeled tour bus pull up at the front entrance!

Approaching its diamond anniversary, the Arizona Inn is undergoing a subtle refurbishing, touch-ups for where 75 years have taken their toll. Doar fairly glowed when she reported that her filmmaker son, Will Conroy, just moved to Tucson from the East Coast with his 10-month-old son Liam. Conroy will assist in planning anniversary events and create a commemorative documentary of the project. So now four generations join in preserving the legacy of hospitality that Greenway began.

Regardless of your day job, savor that legacy for yourself. You'll feel like a Person of Consequence spending time at the inn. The hushed gentility, the strolling pace, the grounds set with inviting lounges and chairs, create a mood. You might feel, as Sir John Wheeler-Bennett wrote after his stay, "cosseted and cherished and made one of the family in these enrapturing conditions."

the value of anachronism

16

Colorado City is a long way from everywhere — in more ways than miles. Tucked away next to iron-red cliffs in Arizona's far northwest corner known as the Arizona Strip, separated from almost everything by the Colorado River coursing through the Grand Canyon, Colorado City sits on the way to practically nothing, unless you have business up in St. George, Utah. Straddling the state's border with its sister city of Hildale, Utah, Colorado City is like the kid in the class who knows he doesn't fit in and sits in the corner hoping not to be noticed. Not that Colorado City isn't proud of what it is. But time has taught that other people have a problem with one father, nine mothers, and dozens of children making up a family unit.

To travel the few paved roads is like going back in time, but with some important details gone awry. The fashions are demurely pioneer, but cars are parked here and there. The businesses are few and far between, but there is communication equipment on the tower near City Hall. The women wear their long hair brushed into elaborate updos, but jeans and running shoes show under some of the long skirts.

Most of the members of the Fundamentalist Church of Jesus Christ of Latter Day Saints live here. To them, the Mormon Church up in Salt

Mayor Dan Barlow of Colorado City: "You can't be half a Saint."

83

Lake City sold out politically, reversing its doctrine on the righteousness of polygamy in order for Utah to gain statehood in the Union. Here, as they have for almost 175 years, men marry, marry, and marry again. Houses are in constant states of expansion. Multiple doors on upper stories indicate partial privacy between wives raising their portions of a family. A raw unfinished place full of potential and machinery, Colorado City revolves around families: homes adding rooms, women buying in bulk at the market, children everywhere. It is like the American Dream interpreted through Alice's looking glass with perhaps a touch of tyranny.

Only eight Mormon prophets since Joseph Smith have led the church in Colorado City. The last two died in their 90s, with around 20 wives each. Every one from now on will have his work cut out for him.

It's been 17 years since I first sat down with Mayor Dan Barlow to talk about his town; as both a church elder and an elected official, he typifies the church-state fusion here; and it is more pleasant each time I do.

The first time was back in the 1980s, when church dissidents were speaking out about dissatisfaction with the United Effort Plan. The church's civic organization that owns most of the land in town, United Effort doles it out to members in good standing. Residents who felt young women were being coerced into marriage had the option of leaving, but with no property to sell and with multiple wives and children, finding someplace to go was difficult.

Outsiders gape when first confronted with plural marriages. Participants remain phlegmatic. "Any man who thinks it sounds great having more than one wife, hasn't tried it," one resident told me on that first trip. Another said, "You know how you can get in trouble without even knowing it with one wife? Well . . ."

And one of the women said, "At least you know where he is at night. Down the hall." (With half of all one-on-one American marriages cracking in two, a successful plural marriage may say much about the power of faith.)

Mayor Barlow was understandably wary of a camera crew full of questions back then. He did say, somewhat formally, that he couldn't understand anyone who would condemn a man "who wants to strengthen his home with two mothers."

He still says that today, and now it's like hearing a high school fight song, pleasantly familiar, new to each graduating class. Colorado City's attitude toward outsiders has changed radically since that early visit: There were no motels in town, and we were even warned to be off the road before dark. Some said local law enforcement had ways of dealing with outsiders on unlit stretches of road that were best avoided. When we did reach our motel in Fredonia, the lights of a patrol car bounced off the walls in eerie unnerving pulses for several hours, just to let us know we were not anonymous.

But since then, the city's general plan has created the goal "to orient people to the etiquette of visiting, what is suitable subject matter for photography or what parts of the community are open to visitors." The town realizes that if townsfolk can't prevent interest, they can at least attempt to channel it.

One of the few places where outlanders and residents mix freely is the Mark Twain Restaurant, its sign visible from the freeway leading into Utah. It hints at a showboat's gaudy allure, luxurious with no thought of restraint, from marble mantels, carved dining booths, and red brocade walls to chandeliers, floral arrangements, and dark wood wainscoting. A young woman in long black skirt and a white Victorian blouse serves a couple clearly just passing through. Dressed to interface with the outside world, a local businessman dines with his wife, whose long curls swing when she bends over the baby in the carrier next to her chair. A group of young men with their elbows on the table all look like young, gangly Jimmy Stewarts, earnest and ready. A patina of health and wholesomeness surrounds the locals, with none of the weary blasé alienation seen in the malls of larger cities.

And Mayor Barlow sits as relaxed and genial as Walt Disney would be showing off his kingdom. He takes time out from a day that has already included meetings and an elementary school dedication to tell my children about the famous "Raid of Short Creek," which was Colorado City's name back in 1953. Governor Howard Pyle, apparently against his better judgment, caved into political pressure and dispatched Department of Public Safety officers to round up men "accused of conspiracy to break the law, by engaging in polygamy."

"I was 21," Barlow explains. "The youngest of my three children was only 10 days old. We had been told they were coming, and we were all rounded up and taken to the old school house. The officers wanted to take the children away, but the mothers insisted on going with them."

Jailed in Kingman with the other men, including bachelors, which Barlow now finds more amusing than upsetting, he had no way of knowing that it would be two years before the U.S. Supreme Court would rule that freedom of religion allowed Short Creek's children to be returned home. Most of the men pleaded guilty to misdemeanor charges and received probation, with the caveat they refrain from practicing polygamy. ("We didn't practice," one resident cracked. "We knew what we were doing.") Barlow calls it "a sad chapter in American history. Even though the government praised us for our industry, they just couldn't stand the religion."

Individual industry may be the strongest ingredient in Colorado City's economy. With few businesses, save a couple of stores and gas stations, hard work on the part of the residents is what keeps the factory operating, the homes and buildings going up, and the crops harvested for sale.

Barlow is proud of the new Mohave Community College branch and of the school he and his brothers established. He reminds me that the airport was proclaimed American Airport of the Year a decade ago and that the school that opened today is a multi-million-dollar K-12 facility.

But of all the civic sites, the one closest to Barlow's heart is Cottonwood Park. Named after a tree so large it won't fit in the average camera's viewfinder, the park just keeps getting better: Besides the miniature railroad and playground facilities that entertain families on weekends and holidays, a zoo now graces the grounds. Barlow tirelessly drives from one end to the other to show off the bear, the elk, the emu, the camel. (The image of a large elk with a splendid rack of antlers leading a dozen or so females seems to fit here perfectly.) He tells about leading a man driving the Caterpillar through the empty fields here years ago, laying out roads to correspond with the vision in his head of the haven for children that exists today.

But it is Colorado City's people, more than its infrastructure, that occupy Barlow's thoughts. He worries about them, as any community leaders do, that the youth will be distracted and tempted by less benign, less productive ways of life than what the parental generation advocates.

"The biggest threat is the liberal world," he says, no different from many parents with radically different religious beliefs. "It turns us away from holy and good principles. Free will is part of our religion; we just believe we teach a better way."

Unlike 20 years ago, when Colorado City's young people, taught that the outside world was cruel and dangerous, never had much chance to find out for themselves, satellite dishes tucked next to woodpiles show how the larger culture intrudes. Options are more available. A few girls we see wear jeans without long skirts over them. The dam has been cracked; the seal has been breached.

But while Barlow wants to be open minded, he doesn't waffle on what is expected.

"You can't be half a Saint," he says firmly. "If you're going to be a Saint, you have got to be a Saint all the way."

(Refreshing; I once saw a cartoon of Einstein saying tentatively, "E equals MC squared — but that could be changed.")

Every so often, Colorado City surfaces on the national radar. Whether allegations of welfare fraud or child abuse, it's made all the more salacious by the accoutrements of everyday life here: the long dresses, the corkscrew curls framing tender faces free of makeup, the high-buttoned shirts, and groups of young men working in fields together. Colorado City residents have, for the most part, learned to keep their eyes lowered and steps rapid when this happens.

But there is always a danger that societal surprise at the mores of this tiny town in its red-dirt pocket of Arizona will become a cause celebre, and religious or social values become pawns.

"Who do you appoint to be the arbiter of other people's religious and moral behavior?" asked a well-spoken woman in Flagstaff discussing this issue. It would be easy to make the jump that if a teenage girl is forced into marriage, the system must be changed.

But I recently read a book about a period of American history right after the Revolutionary War, where "Regulators" rebelled against the new country's upper class, which was getting property in bankruptcy sales and profiting on others' misfortunes. Not only is it interesting that mention of this is assiduously avoided in our schools, but it underlines a larger point: The idea that individuals were greedy or cruel does not mean the concept of democracy was a bust.

Polygamy may carry hazards. Any philosophy, once touched by humans, is vulnerable to corruption. But if you drive down one of the dirt roads between burgeoning homes surrounded by playground equipment and gardens, seeing the healthy bright-haired children vigorously riding bikes or holding younger siblings' hands, it's clear that many things here work better than in most cities.

Colorado City is that vanishing breed of American community: somewhere different than most places. It will be a delicate tightrope walk to keep the values intact while popular culture presses in around the edges. If Mayor Barlow has his way, faith and tradition will guide the steps of the people here.

down mexico way

17

Exaggerated statuary advertised restaurants in Amado and Carmen on I-19 south of Tucson.

They used to call it *El Camino del Muerto*, "the road of death." The two-lane road, stretching from the twin border towns of Nogales, Arizona, and Nogales, Mexico, north to Tucson, brought back tourists who had purchased duty-free liquor south of the border, imbibed numerous margaritas with their lunches in Mexico, and then hopped back in their cars to head home. Naturally, that single stretch could account for more drunk driving accidents than most other highways in Arizona.

But tougher laws, the wider Interstate 19, and perhaps better sense (have you noticed how many people drink less these days?) — have dimmed the road's nefarious reputation, letting the more interesting merits of nature, culture, and history shine through.

Leaving Tucson and heading south to Nogales, one of the first sights worth seeing is the "White Dove of the Desert," the Mission San Xavier del Bac. Both historical landmark, as one of Father Eusebio Kino's missions dating back to 1700, and active parish for the Tohono O'odham Indian tribe, San Xavier seen from the road seems to glow white.

Farther on, Duval Mine Road leads off to the Titan Missile Museum, which my brother Lyle considers one of Arizona's more significant historical sites. The Cold War, while it may seem benign compared to today's terrorism, really wasn't. Remember the Doomsday Clock, which calculated how long it would take to totally destroy the world with nuclear weapons? As other museums help us see why we should say, "Never again," the tunnel deep into the ground that used to hold death and destruction in a ready-to-launch tube sobers you while it also refreshes your perspective. We can still take comfort in the great adage, "We ain't what we should be, and we ain't what we could be, but thank God, we ain't what we was."

It isn't until you've driven past the retirement community of Green Valley that local color really pushes up through. The community of Amado carries the name of one of the early pioneer families that came up from Mexico. At the Arivaca exit, you can spot two quirky restaurants. The Longhorn, which has cycled through many names over the years, never forsook its cow skull facade, complete with mammoth steer horns curving above. Don't be intimidated, but you have to enter through the skull's "mouth." Across the street is what I thought was the original Cow Palace, until I went to San Francisco as an adult. I remember having lunch there with a photographer who looked at the description of liquor-laced Arizona coffee and remarked, "That'd set you free." I hope tourists don't think that's how Arizonans generally take coffee.

Between Arivaca and Tubac, you can see the formation of Elephant

Head on your left. Depending on the time of day, the rock jutting out from the Santa Rita range looks only vaguely like an elephant head or uncannily just like one. It's all in the light and play of shadow.

Tubac, a thriving artists community, also has my favorite cemetery in the state, because it reflects the mix of Anglo and Hispanic cultures that swirl together here. Curving wrought iron letters over the entrance proclaim it the "Tubac Cementary," combining the Spanish *cementaria* and our own similar word. This is the cheeriest set of burial plots I've ever seen, as full of life as of death: bright flowers, lovingly maintained monuments, permanent vases on plots that are always crowded by other arrangements. Families still use it, and someday it would be fun to come on *El Dia del Muerte*, the Mexican celebration of "the Day of the Dead" on Nov. 1. I bet it teems with visitors cleaning and feasting.

Tubac's charming chapel, called St. Ann's, stands humble but perfect next to the old Spanish presidio (where the first newspaper in Arizona was published).

From here, on the frontage road, Mexican Catholic culture abounds. Even though the homes are humble, shrines dot the side of the road. One — I can remember it seeing over the years since I was small — stands up on the west, with stairs leading to the grotto where the Virgin of Guadalupe statue gazes out over the land. Another shrine at ground level on the east is an actual room, its sliding glass door open a bit to let in the electric cord for the light illuminating the statue of Mary inside.

Tumacacori, the preserved ruins of another Kino mission, is on your left. Right before it, in a town called Carmen, is another landmark restaurant, Wisdom's Café.

You know how remembering something from your childhood makes it loom larger: Hills were steeper than when you go back to see them from an adult's eye level? Well, the plaster chickens in front of Wisdom's Café — huge birds in my memory — turn out to be only person-high. A little disturbing since I came here throughout my 20s, but there you are. The grandson of the original owner says that, in the 1940s, a man who leased the restaurant for a brief time called it the Chicken Taco and added the barnyard friends. They remained after the family took it over again. He speaks while his tiny daughter romps around and then takes her out back for her nap. The whole family still lives in a compound of homes behind the restaurant. I leave, wishing more of that kind of thing were happening in the bigger cities.

Scattered across the high grassland between here and the border, stretching toward Sonoita, spread ranches, many owned by old Arizona families. I stayed at several long ago and was enchanted by a lifestyle I thought had long since disappeared. Guest rooms opened off the central courtyard; the furnishings were Mexican and antique and colorful. Dogs frolicked in the courtyard and neighbors pulled up in pickups to call out that if we wanted anything, they were headed to town. Everyone gathered for dinner and played board games afterward in salas and libraries and great rooms with fires glowing on the hearth.

At one, the Wingfield Ranch, pictures of "the Duke" were numerous. I didn't stay in the John Wayne bedroom, but he probably swam in the lapis lazuli pool we used.

Driving back up, it occurred to me that while the Arizona Strip north of the Grand Canyon almost seems to belong to Utah more than to Arizona, this landscape of rugged mountains and rolling grasslands at the state's southern edge almost seems more part of Mexico. Religion as a part of everyday life, the strong family ties, and the bright primary splashes of color give it a flavor far different from the rest of the state.

It continues to vividly remind us of Arizona's roots, the mix of Anglo and Mexican cultures, which in turn had been mixed by Spaniards and local Indian tribes. It is the quintessential sharing of diversity and, as such — a virtual road of life — it eclipses any road of death.

stitching the honeymoon trail

18

While the early Spanish explorers and Catholic padres mapped and explored what is now Arizona, we owe much of our state's history in the northern and eastern regions to the Church of Jesus Christ of Latter-day Saints. Persecuted and hounded from back East and through the Midwest, the early Mormons set their sights on the sanctuary of the remote West, many trudging across the continent on foot to follow their prophet, Brigham Young. The isolated Arizona Strip, sandwiched by Utah and the Colorado River, is steeped in Mormon pioneer settlement, which

Pipe Springs
National
Monument
displays indoor
and outdoor
relics.

93

also seeps over the river toward eastern Arizona. Threads of Mormon influence don't disappear; they appear again in other sites on the tapestry of our heritage.

One such thread surfaces at Pipe Spring north of the Grand Canyon and southwest of Fredonia. Settlers built the fortified complex — which become known as Winsor Castle — at Brigham Young's behest in 1870. The site gave the young church somewhere to raise the cattle that were often part of the 10 percent tithe required of every Saint. Cannily designed to actually cover the spring so that no enemy could cut off or poison the water that sustained the land, this defendable fortress never needed to use the gun slots built into the stone walls.

Pipe Spring's oasis on the high grassland of the Colorado Plateau welcomed many travelers in the latter years of the 19th century. John Wesley Powell stayed there before starting on his famous surveying trip of the Grand Canyon. Now a national monument, Pipe Spring offers an active look at frontier Arizona life, from the heavy iron stove with the warming oven up top, where tiny babies slept safe from the chill, to the gardens growing vegetables that young visitors can pick and feed to the ponies stabled there. The spring still fills a welcoming pond out front and cools the stone rooms where the original dairy equipment still stands.

Besides supplying butter, cheese, and cattle to the Mormon population in St. George, Utah, Pipe Spring became a relay station for the Deseret Telegraph even before construction was complete. Eliza Louella Stewart, a young and independent Mormon who was a career girl ahead of her time, operated the telegraph, the only system in this area. With the desk and telegraph equipment she used still sitting under a window at Pipe Spring, it's easy to imagine dark-haired Eliza earnestly at work sending messages.

The next time you may encounter mention of Eliza is further east, in St. Johns. She married and became one of two wives of David King Udall, the patriarch who may have contributed more descendents to the United States Congress than any other man.

(The St. Johns cemetery yielded some of my own family's Mormon history. My great-grandmother, Sedona, came west with her husband, T.C. Schnebly, at the behest of his brother, D.E. Neither my father nor his sisters knew where D.E. ended up after he drifted away from Oak Creek Canyon. When I went to St. Johns to do a story about Morris "Mo" Udall, the venerable Arizona congressman, we were at the cemetery shooting video of headstones in the Udall plot. In the row behind them was a stone reading "D.E. and Mary Schnebly: Teachers." This, then, was where the wandering brother's path concluded.)

The chain of eastern Arizona towns established by Mormons — Winslow, Heber, Snowflake, Eager, St. Johns — all contributed to the existence of the Honeymoon Trail. In the Mormon church's early years out west, couples wanting to be officially joined for eternity had to travel to the temple in St. George, Utah. That meant an arduous journey up over what was called "Hell's Backbone," an unforgiving trail paralleling the Vermilion Cliffs and crossing the Colorado River at Lee's Ferry.

Emma Lee ran the ferry regularly in the 1870s, since her husband John was off scouting and surveying for the church. Ultimately, he was shot into his own coffin for the Mountain Meadow Massacre, a regrettable chapter in Mormon history up in St. George.

Ten years after Lee's execution, Emma married a man named Frank French and made her home in Winslow. She filled a local niche as midwife; her home became known as "The Baby Farm." Since many women lived out on homesteads, with husbands who were cowboys or ranchers or railroaders who might not be home when labor began, women planned ahead to stay in town with Emma through their delivery. Winslow was largely a railroad town, and men who worked on the Santa Fe Railroad paid extra when they could for women to assist Emma in caring for their wives and new infants.

Emma Lee French's work as a healer became legendary in part because of an incident where a barroom brawl left one man shot in the lung and the other sliced virtually to ribbons. The sheriff didn't think he'd have to wait long for one to die and to charge whichever one temporarily survived, but someone summoned Emma. She removed the bullet and stitched the other man together over several hours. Within two weeks, the men had become buddies and were drinking side by side at the saloon again. Emma died in 1897 with everyone, from prostitutes to ranch wives to lawmen, gathered in vigil at her home.

Another one of the patches in the quilt of Mormon-Arizona history picks up threads back at Lee's Ferry. Maybe 20 graves penned inside a wire fence, the cemetery there is as humble a resting place as I've ever seen, set against the symphonic, full-choir, angel-inspired background of the Vermilion Cliffs. Scrubby grass and unmarked stones are elevated to message-saturated scenery against the deep russet, rose, and rust crags and crofts of the soaring stone.

Here, four Johnson children were laid to rest, all in a line and within a tragically short time. Walking past the markers, mentally subtracting years to get ages, you note that Jonathan was 5; Laura Alice, 7; Permilia, 9; and Melinda, 15, that hot, early summer of 1891 when they all died of diphtheria within a five-week span.

A passing family had lost a son to an unknown illness at Panguitch, Utah. Sorrowing themselves, they must have thought it a kindness, when they used the ferry to cross the river, to leave some of his clothing and blankets for the 11 children of the family living there. Who knew that diphtheria would spread to the unsuspecting recipients? The National History Association office at Lee's Ferry has two photographs of the Johnson family, one before and one taken some time after the deaths. Mrs. Johnson looks harsh and defeated in the second.

The wonderful weaving strands of history pick up the pattern again farther west in Colorado City. The baby in the Johnson family photograph was Leroy, who grew up to become the leader of that polygamist town. "Uncle Roy" Johnson, always seeming a bit stern in the news photos, was Colorado City's revered patriarch until he died in 1990. Gnarled and indomitable, he wasn't a sympathetic figure, but to see him as the sturdy child once seated on his mother's knee puts him in a softer light.

In 1953, when the Arizona Department of Public Safety raided Colorado City, then called Short Creek, for its widespread polygamy, Mormon families across eastern Arizona fostered the children removed from their polygamist families. The Honeymoon Trail no longer existed, but the towns that marked it, like stars in a constellation, still looked after their own.

resisting daylight-saving time

19 I never feel so much like an Arizonan as when I read a mention about daylight-saving time.

Periodically, we Arizonans are urged to adopt the system, but "They just want us to be like the rest of 'em," I think, and "We'll change our clocks when they pry them out of our cold, dead fingers." I feel mulish and stubborn. But behind that, I don't want to be manipulated into trying to impress the rest of the nation with our progressiveness, when I know it won't work. Not this way.

We've been urged to "join the rest of the country" and "come into the 21st century" by doing the "spring forward, fall back" ballet with the other states, artificially creating, then revoking, an hour each April and October. That's akin to a good funeral salesman asking, "Don't you want your mother to be comfortable for eternity?" Well, to say no would be churlish. It isn't that we don't want to be with the rest of the country, or that we don't want to live in the 21st century (well, sometimes we don't want to, but we're here, and that's that), but you don't show unity with someone by being at 9 o'clock together. Cooperation is deeper, and more difficult, than that.

When it comes to time, Arizona eschews resetting it twice a year.

Every year, Tuba City shows up in at least a sidebar story on one of the daylight-saving switch days as a pocket of a place out of time in Arizona. The Navajo Nation, extending as it does into Utah and New Mexico, officially uses daylight-saving time. So Tuba City changes its clocks twice a year and confuses passing Grand Canyon tourists and Flagstaff businesses making calls. But you don't read as frequently about Arizona Strip residents along the Utah border, who unofficially live by Utah time.

I don't think changing to daylight-saving time will make anyone happy except the stockbrokers who have to get up three hours early to stay in touch with Wall Street's opening bell (although they wouldn't be done so soon, would they?). I think if we labor under the delusion that we can give Arizona some happy press in the nation's eyes by going along on this, it's like thinking we can put a bully with horrible manners in a sharp shirt and get other kids to like him.

Our state's public spending on mental health care and our financing for schools and children's programs are a national disgrace. We have been a laughingstock for electing, then rejecting, more than one scandal-ridden governor.

(We voted dumb. It's over. Let's get past it. We should remember from the playground that you can't wheedle and whine someone into liking you. Enough explaining. Let's handle our business without tap dancing. It's our state, and we pay the price for our decisions.)

Arizona is, to our credit, ruggedly individual to the point of being contentious. That's how the West was won — people who couldn't cut it in the East, who didn't like obeying rules or didn't play well with other children, came here. No questions asked, no credentials necessary. (I was well into adulthood before a woman from somewhere else actually asked me, "Who are your people?" Out here, that just isn't done.) So the attitude of "But everyone else does it this way" doesn't carry much weight in our state.

Better for tourism, some say, to go to daylight-saving time. But no matter where you go, someone must always adjust to time differences, since time zones exist across the country whether the clock is set back or not. Besides, we would confuse tourists who are used to being on the same time as California during the summer traveling months. Why screw that up?

The counter argument that we get quite enough summer sunshine, thank you, makes sense to me. Tourists and residents alike would despair at postponing the blessed relief of sunset yet another hour. Besides, when you switch back in October — when days are already naturally short-ening — it's like getting spanked by darkness to suddenly bring it an hour sooner.

And tourists don't come for the time zone; they come for the flavor. This is a quirky state with dry washes rather than rivers and road signs for spots like Bloody Basin and Hell's Canyon. This is a state with real live cowboys who walk stiff. And spit in public. Point is, you can't pretty up something without changing it. If we pumped water into our washes to make visitors feel at home, if we served milder chili, would we really be giving people what they want? What about what we want?

I think the real point is to avoid jockeying for acceptance from other states. If we want approval, we should address issues of import: our treat-ment of immigrants, our state spending on health and education. Going to daylight-saving time means little more than a cosmetic concession that wouldn't correct anything but impressions.

To see the light and change your mind about something is laudable. To act differently from your true self, hoping people will approve of you, is wrong.

If Arizona needs an image polish, let's not just shine a brighter light on the status quo with hopes of making it sparkle. Let's fix whatever's broken. Bleating in tune with one's neighbors doesn't make one better. Just more of a sheep.

20

The land of the Navajo — or the Diné, as they refer to themselves — spreads spare and powerful, a vast space where God seems to have stored relics from an amalgam of other terrains: a long bluff, full of lavender and sienna shades; a series of tiny alkaline washes that offer miniature lessons in how water and wind carved out the Grand Canyon; a series of lumped mounds that look like a forgotten, otherworldly village.

It's odd to see orderly electrical towers, looking like kachina dolls interpreted by Picasso, connected by wires so they won't stray in this strange country. Tiny seeps show up as pockets of green, frequently with a hogan nearby. But natural scenery, more than human enterprise, dominates this country. Except in Cameron.

I say "in" instead of "at," even though Cameron's main drag numbers little more than one set of buildings, because one building is a post office. Hovering on the lip of the Little Colorado River Gorge, the Cameron Trading Post embodies so much more than a store. It is an empire, including an RV park, gallery, food store, restaurant, lodge, and landscaped courtyard.

The original building at Cameron Trading Post portrays rugged tradition.

While the trading post looks old, it's not all original. The dining room's pressed and patterned tin ceilings hark back to the era of the first trading post — which opened in 1916 — but these were shipped in from back East during a fairly recent renovation. The elaborately bricked garden paths, stairs, and arches look like a hidden oasis from long ago, but stacks of brick and branches show evidence of current work. And while some of the Navajo rugs, jewelry, and crafts could have been made a century ago, again, there's a modern improvement: You can find them all available on-line.

Call up camerontradingpost.com at your leisure. What a journey! The outpost that once took days to reach by lurching wagon or tiring horse is now the touch of a few fingertips away. And while the early traders may have flung a bedroll down in the shade of the building, the website describes not only motel rooms, but luxury suites, complete with wet bars and lounging areas. Forget cowboy coffee in the tin can over the fire — your room boasts a coffee maker. By clicking on "gardens" on the Web site, you not only get a view of the floral abundance and flagstone terraces, but are presented with the idea that these same environs would be perfect for a wedding or reunion.

The juxtaposition of rugged tradition and slick marketing may be a little unnerving for some. You can forget the modern edge walking into the wide dining room, with its antique display cabinets, spindled chairs, and glorious view. Utensils are simple, and the menu is nicely devoid of anything with beurre blanc or mango salsa.

Navajo tacos, those sumptuous billows of fried dough layered with beans, seasoned meat, and fixin's, are a specialty of the house. There is also a fine old rural Arizona tradition: pie available at breakfast. Somehow the only offering I wouldn't want was the latte. When in Rome, maybe. But not here.

The original purpose of a trading post was shopping for provisions, and while other accoutrements have been added, shopping remains a priority. You can wander through the aisles of what is essentially a grocery store, although you can't buy a fresh chicken. This flows seamlessly into the trading post's main area, which offers something for everyone, from the plentiful bargains of arrowheads by the dish, to cloth dolls with molded faces, to quite significant sculptures and carvings at prices to match. Postcard, pot holder, squash-blossom jewelry, carved fetish — you'll find them all here.

The high rollers of buying native go next door to the gallery, which has true fine art, whether woven, inlaid, or carved. Few people are seen passing through the fine heavy doors of the old building to the gallery, but many plunk down a charge card and carry out a cumbersome metal Kokopelli in wild paint, a petroglyph t-shirt or hat, or a Native American music CD.

I was tempted by a sale shelf of china imprinted with the Cameron Trading Post basket and name — plates and saucers at rock-bottom prices. Envisioning a Thanksgiving table graced with these distinctive celebrations of our state's history, I was crushed to see them labeled "for display only; not intended for food." I bought one plate anyway.

From most of the rooms, in a handy melding of nature's artwork and man's additions, the panorama of the Little Colorado River Gorge can be seen extending in both directions. The gorge's bridge may not be the original swaying span put up in 1911, but it's old enough that my father remembers driving across it — only one car at a time, in either direction — in the 1930s. He points out how it's higher at the north end than the south and describes how he and his sisters would gather the biggest flattest stones they could find, if they were heading north. Dropping rocks off the Navajo Bridge over the Colorado River farther north was such fun that the ground around that bridge had been already picked clean of the best dropping rocks. So Cameron gave up its bounty.

One man can take the most credit for the Cameron Trading Post's coming of age. Joe Atkinson, the current owner, comes from a long line of Indian traders and entrepreneurs, and he has set about to make a good thing better without losing its rustic appeal. He's done a darn fine job — the food is good, the employees appear local and competent. You can get Lorna Doone cookies in a tiny six-pack or a handwoven Navajo

wool rug for thousands of dollars, and many other items, whether lux-
uries or essentials, in between.

While it seems a bit muddled to be able to get all this over the Web,
I guess it is true to the original spirit of the trading post. At that time,
trading post owners lived on or near the reservations and learned how
to provide the local tribes with what they needed, taking in turn what
was offered. While not always bosom buddies, successful trading post
owners were trusted enough to hold pawned jewelry until the agreed
time, to take and deliver personal messages, and to give fair value for
jewelry or rugs brought to barter. They did what they had to do to make
things work for their customers. So Joe Atkinson, like any good trader,
is working within the customer's abilities and expectations: giving them
a home page. Heritage dot com.

You can log on, see the gallery, read about the scenery, and learn
some of the history. But even virtual tours have limits. I will stop making that fairly long drive up to Cameron Trading Post only when I can
get a Navajo taco delivered fresh to my computer desk. With pie.

a street runs through it

21

Downtown
Flagstaff shows
its vintage
character with a
Babbitt's sign
and the
Weatherford
Hotel's balcony.

Few things manage to be as simultaneously ugly and charming as downtown Flagstaff.

If you drive up from under the railroad bridge and go a few blocks north anywhere, you will see houses of great appeal cheek-by-jowl with old tired ones. Handsomely restored commercial buildings share curb space with some leftover mid-20th-century boxes that never had distinction to lose. In winter, the landscape languishes in shades of wet ash and dull brown, tinged with cinder dust from the railroad tracks.

But even on its worst day, downtown Flagstaff's picturesque stretches redeem its lesser sites. It's somewhat like a woman who may have a space between her front teeth, a deep voice, and wide hands, but possesses such splendid red hair and joie de vivre that the flaws become part of a striking portrait.

Flagstaff somehow manages to keep its history current. Many of the pressed-tin ceilings still glow with a vintage patina. Advertising painted on the brick walls may be fading, but the ads haven't been covered over. The building that housed the bakery when it had a one-digit phone number looks much as it did 60 years ago, when my father, at age 9, would bike over before breakfast to fetch the family's daily loaf of bread.

When we were children, we would visit what is now the bar in the Weatherford Hotel, and my parents would point out where my father was sitting, eating sardines, when he asked my mother out on their first date, more than a half-century ago. The Weatherford was already historic then, because of Zane Grey having written there and other early luminaries having lodged upstairs. Now, a photo of environmental writer Edward Abbey hoisting a pint in the same pub adds a new generation of historical presence. The Weatherford actually looks better than it has in years, with the white second-floor balcony and bunting over the entrance.

The years must have brought a high volume of celebrity traffic through Flagstaff, because over at the Monte Vista Hotel, the early guest registers also boast august signatures: Zane Grey, again, who must have liked to spread the wealth; Clark Gable; John Wayne. With its arched windows and brick façade, the Monte Vista could be superimposed upon a 1930s photograph and not startle the viewer.

The northern Arizona news bureau for the Phoenix station KTVK occupies space there. Mike Schmidt and I used to climb to the roof to do live shots overlooking the city. It always felt somewhat secret, like children sneaking into the rafters to go above where the elevator cables wheezed and toiled and out onto the silver tar-paper expanse, with views in all directions: Cherry Hill, with some of the prettiest old homes anywhere, each completely individual. The small house where my father first keyed a microphone to say, "This is KWRZ, Flagstaff," and discovered he would be an announcer the rest of his life. The darling train depot where we used to go meet my grandparents. The gorgeous Church of the Blessed Virgin Mary, with its incongruous gargoyles. Looking out over the familiar buildings brought a satisfaction of *Our Town* caliber, an awareness of the preciousness of here and now.

Across from the Monte Vista is the Babbitt Building, one of the refurbished originals from Flagstaff's early days. The Babbitt family helped develop Flagstaff, and Flagstaff and the Babbitt name should always be inextricably linked. Just up the street, across from the Inn at 410, is the childhood home of Bruce Babbitt, former Arizona governor and once secretary of the interior.

Beaver Street is the lodgepole of downtown, connecting it to the Northern Arizona University campus. Walking across the tracks (everything is accompanied by the sound track of occasional train whistles), you get to Macy's. The coffeehouse has expanded since it opened in one room, but it has not lost any of its alpine sincerity. Muffins the size of bowling balls and matchless coffee drinks, even though everyone seems to have entered the coffee game, are better because the very air seems healthy inside.

Across the street is the Beaver Street Brew Pub, which has many past lives. The building opened as Food Town 60-odd years ago. My father remembers excited townsfolk buzzing about the fact that the store would sell ice cream, which you could buy and take home! All the time! No need to make it yourself or go to a drugstore with a soda fountain. And the free samples at the grand opening made an impression on him that has endured. Then later, as a young head resident of NAU's Peterson Hall, my father shopped there for his small family. The structure slumped, resorting to selling used goods for a time, but was reborn about a decade ago as the alehouse and restaurant. Now the memories are of fondue dinners after rafting the Canyon and watching my children dance as the band plays in the courtyard. The walls of Beaver Street Brew Pub must be so saturated in memory quilts such as ours that it probably keeps the place warm in winter.

Best of all to me is the fact that downtown is not preserved as an exhibit, but puts its historic charm to full daily use. Dogs wait happily for masters between bicycles on the sidewalks; bulletin boards rotate notices for concerts, meetings, and exhibits. And you don't need your car.

I used to walk down Leroux Street to Café Espress and buy a delectable peanut butter cookie and a cup of coffee. Carrying these, I could stroll over to buy stamps at the post office, then stop in at the copy store with a letter I wanted duplicated. I could duck across the street to get my hair trimmed and be back in 10 minutes, buy gloves at the outdoor shops, and walk to the bank. You could drive to the mall, but you didn't always need to.

Flagstaff's downtown straddles past and present. New businesses move in without eradicating what came before. One of the joys of growing older is being able to add layers of recollections that rise up when seeing the familiar places again. Downtown Flagstaff is the dark scent of roasting coffee, the vigor of young window shoppers, and, always, the poignant serenade of train whistles.

keylee's hometown

22

Keylee King, left, with her mother, Kathy Schaeffer; grandmother, Linda Camp; and great-grandmother, Kristina Smith.

Lake Havasu City is where Keylee lives. You haven't heard of Keylee King, yet. But you might.

I met her when I was leading a writing group consisting of girls who were having a hard time merging onto society's freeway. They would have been classified as "troubled," but they were also creative, vulnerable, and full of dreams. We met once a week to do writing exercises, discuss issues, and share our work. I don't know about them, but it was the some of the most informative, moving, important times I've ever had.

JUNE

Keylee didn't seem at first like someone who would put a town on the map the way Sinatra did Hoboken, or Elvis did Memphis. She is small, with nutmeg-colored hair and eyes like espresso. She brightly taught me the language she knew: that your teeth are your "grill," that "kickin' it" is spending time together, and that "curb-crunching" is when you make someone lie in the street and bite the curb, then kick the back of her head — whether hard enough to dislodge a few teeth or snap the spine is up to the cruncher, not the crunchee. Not that she ever did that. But she had grown up in a much harsher environment than I.

Still, that was only one facet of the girl who loved green, got breathlessly choked up over a compliment, and was always passionate in her views. She came in one time, glowing with excitement because she'd discovered the poem "The Raven" and wanted us all to get to revel in Poe's language, meter, and images. And her writing! It took my breath away.

Once, when Afghanistan was in the news, I brought in a newspaper photo of women hooded in burquas, riding in a cart. We discussed what it would be like to inhabit a shell of cloth wherever we went. The girls viewed it somewhat differently than I had: A woman behind a burqua was safe was their primary reaction. And that those women weren't regarded as sexual fodder, nor were they required to please men by how they dressed.

Their assignment was to write a first-person account of how it would feel to be the woman behind the burqua. Keylee's began: "The fog of fabric floats from my wisdom to my walk." I was intellectually smitten, the way I am when any writer, from Edward Abbey to Edna St. Vincet Millay, voices something so perfectly that it is instantly preserved in the amber of my mind.

On another assignment, Keylee decided to take on her last prejudice, anti-Semitism. (She had already moved on from her early indoctrination in racism, homophobia, and fundamentalism, so she felt ready to slay this final dragon.) She wrote about a photograph of men looking out from a concentration camp and picked one of the faces to give voice to.

Her piece spoke of feeling overpowered to respond to the SS troops, who come waving their flags with their horrible symbols of hate. She got past the specifics of religion to the emptiness of being told by a larger society that you are worthless and deserving of hate. Her triumphant polemic against the oppressors has not yet been read by anyone without tears.

Keylee embodies the delicate alchemy of unusual thoughts and unusual language in which to frame them. She may end up taking a few college courses, amusing her friends throughout her life with clever letters at the holidays, and keeping great journals that will be a future archivist's heaven and hell.

Or she may be emboldened enough to put some of the words out in the world — shyly at first, the way she brought them to us, but with the enthusiasm that makes real writers simply have to write, and having written, share. I have never been in the presence of a talent such as hers before it reached a mass market. I think I know how Abraham Lincoln's teacher, or songwriter Don Henley's neighbor, may have felt: "This is a brilliant soul disguised as a regular person. I wonder how much of it will come out."

I got to see Keylee recently and to meet her mother, grandmother, and great-grandmother, all living in Lake Havasu. I also met two very protective male friends, who sobered me with tales of some exploits at a recent party. (I sometimes forget how rough is the diamond.) She was actually a little afraid I would be disappointed that so far she not only doesn't have an agent, but she hasn't written anything significant for a few months. I told her not to worry about that; just stay sane and in control, and she will come to realize that all her experiences are fodder — compost, if you will — which will coalesce into a rich loam to nourish the seeds of her writing. Someday, people may go to Lake Havasu City and see the London Bridge, walk the paths around the water, and probably shop. Then they'll want to drive by the house that boasts a modest plaque saying this was where Keylee King lived back in the 1990s.

Which raises the question of fame versus worth. If her childhood home never makes the National Register, will her talent have been wasted? How many people must make up an audience for a work to be considered successful — more than a hundred? What if it's only one person who is awed and amazed and never stops marveling at the words? If you've changed one person forever, even if only yourself, does that count for as much as mildly amusing 10,000 for a few minutes?

I don't know the answers. But to me, Lake Havasu City is the hometown of Keylee King.

Cynthia Billings
and Dennis Harris
take rafters
down the
Colorado River.

death at river mile 76

23

The first step is the biggest. Sloshing through the Colorado River's shockingly cold water onto the motorized raft at Lee's Ferry, thoughts of a quick call from the dilapidated pay phone may cross one's mind. After all, once you board and drift from shore, you are in a rare position in today's society: stuck. For good or ill, the next eight days and 225 miles are in many ways out of your control. Which is why you've come.

Seven of us had planned this Grand Canyon rafting trip together; the other 10 people in the party were strangers. From rafting years before, we had learned this was part of the delight: People you would normally never speak to, out of either intimidation or boredom, turn out to have fascinating things to say. So we pulled into the river's gentle jade current, ready to create a small but fully functional organized floating community.

Dennis Harris, the boatman, becomes for a spell our captain, town manager, and patriarch. Joking about how some people complain immediately upon discovering their welfare is in the hands of a man who hasn't cut his hair since the mid-1980s, he handles the rudder easily without even looking. Some 150 trips like this have given him all the confidence he needs to deliver us safely to Diamond Creek. Cynthia Billings is first mate and first lady — as frisky and strong as a colt, with what my brother calls calico hair: auburn, honey, gold, cocoa, floating long and free from under her sun visor down to the waistband of her sarong. She exudes enthusiasm; the smallest helpful gesture on the part of a passenger, like filling a water bucket, is met with a hearty, "You rock!"

The rest of us are stories yet to be shared, first impressions that will be reinforced, and altered, at varying times during the week. Still with our cultural game faces, we start throwing out tentative disclosures like the first hesitant cards in a poker game. Someone is afraid the hikes will be too hard. Someone else is worried a cat back home in New York won't be fed. I brought a mirror.

Common wisdom holds that it takes three days to hit your stride on the Colorado River. On the ride up, four people have had their cell phones working. Gradually, the stake in the outside world falls away. But our second day, I find out my brother and I are both still mentally calculating miles: At the rate we're going, we don't have any built-in pad. We must make better time! Intellectually, we understand Dennis is aware of what must be done, but the deadline mentality we've brought is not as easily packed away as my cute but tractionless boat shoes.

Sunday, the third day, things are jelling. Carrying buckets down to the water for dishwashing, I realize I'm smiling out of the pure pleasure of being in this place. Walking to the bank under an arch of tamarisk and willow branches, with the endless music of the Colorado, the preternaturally blue sky, and no responsibilities save returning with a full bucket of water, I am completely content. As much as I love my home and family, I am not often completely content doing morning dishes. I savor the feeling.

Maybe because I'm now adapted, I become more curious about fellow passengers. We've already taken my favorite hike; I've dreamed for 15 years about seeing Saddle Canyon again. So it was startling to hear Cindy, a veterinarian from Alabama, say upon seeing the thin ribbon of silver falls at Saddle, "We came all that way for this?" That evening at camp, just above River Mile 76, I'm spreading clean laundry on a rock (although clean is a relative term; a little Ivory soap and the 45-degree water, and you figure sun and scrubbing sand will do the rest) next to where Cindy is writing in a notebook. I ask if she journals; we begin to talk. She has endured the worst experience of her life only weeks ago. She and a companion were hit by a car; he may never recover fully. "I never want to go through anything like that again," she says.

That's when we hear the shout. I don't even know if it sounded like, "Help!" but we look at one another in alarm. As we move toward the beach, we see a man, floating down the river by the cliff wall about a hundred yards away. Only his head is visible. Then he goes under. Dimly I recall having seen a man fishing off a rock ledge just up the river on that side. As we begin to digest what must have happened, Dennis and Cynthia have already leaped on the raft, untying as they go. Mike, a 22-year-old from Pennsylvania, and Paul, a New York television director who used to be a volunteer firefighter in Long Island, jump onto the raft as it pulls into the current. Cindy begins to shake. I pull her close and start to pray.

"Dear Lord, be with that man. Be with our crew, and help them do Your work here." We watch, riveted, with others from our group who had been drawn from camp activities. Dennis has headed downriver.

117

"That guy is up here! He's going too far!" Cindy protests.

I say the smartest thing I'll say the whole trip: "Dennis knows what he's doing."

(Later, I hear Dennis describe to National Park Service investigators how he happened to be at the right place to rescue the man: "At that point, the current is along the right bank, then it cuts about a 45-degree angle across and swirls and eddies where we went. I knew I had to have passed him.")

Sure enough, we see a burst of movement on the boat. "They've got him!" someone yells. After starting to wonder if anyone could have survived this long in water so cold you get brain freeze washing your hair, we breathe a collective sigh of relief. We wait for the cough, the movement. Surely he will now say, "That was close!" and head back to his camp with a good story.

But instead, the intense and driven gestures of CPR begin. We watch the force in Mike's muscles as he tries to get a heartbeat. We see the focus of every line in every body on that boat as Dennis heads upstream. We have a veterinarian and a registered nurse at camp, he's remembered. Both Cindy and Patti are ready to climb on board before the boat even reaches our beach.

As anyone who has witnessed a car accident knows, waiting and watching feels horrible. We continue to pray, alone and in groups.

"God, I know You know what You're doing," I say. "But if there's any wiggle room on this one, please bring him back. Please bring him back."

The CPR continues as the boat angles back upriver, fighting the inexorable current with everything a talented boatman and a 30-horsepower motor can do. Dennis reaches the beach where the man had slipped off and bounds up the rock cliff like a mountain goat, only holding his satellite phone. He's going to get help. Somewhere in here, members of the man's group arrive. Other guides start trying to reach a satellite with their emergency phones. On the boat, the relentless CPR doesn't flag or dim. It is heartbreaking to watch; obviously, they wouldn't be repeating the desperate exercise so long if they had been successful in bringing him back.

Around the time the helicopter came in, most of us were shifting our prayer. We began talking about how this would be a perfect place to die, if it were one's time. We wondered if the body on the boat was only a shell being watched by the person who had inhabited it and if he felt compassion and tenderness for the crew of rescuers who were not giving up, who would not give up, this long and exhausting hour and more, until they could no longer reach him.

First we heard the rotor blades of the chopper, then saw it swing into view downriver and head toward us, red lights flashing like a lighthouse in the gathering dark. It was an odd sensation, like stepping into an episode of "M*A*S*H," when "Incoming!" is a harbinger of hard things. The chopper pilot reached the bend in the river where Dennis had stopped the raft, and we presumed radio communication was going on while the pilot gauged wind gusts and the feasibility of landing; first by the raft, then on another beach across the river.

Like displaced children wanting to help their parents in a crisis, our group had started potatoes baking, brought warm clothes down to the beach, and finished setting up tents. Then, from across the river, came a shout, "Clear the camp! The chopper needs to land!"

We knew the rotors would create a tremendous updraft to suck anything not anchored down, so we tore to the edge of the campsite by the water. Tents and bags, already weighted down with rocks against the river wind, were hurled into the ridge of tamarisk trees. Later we found out we'd broken lotion bottles, ruined possessions. But we battened down in the bushes and watched the helicopter move and hover, seemingly dangerously close. The raft slid across the river, holding position against the current, and several from our group leaped forward to help carry the metal table that had become a gurney off the bobbing raft to the helicopter.

My brother Lindsay was one of those. Later, he told me, "I've never washed a dying man's blood off my hands before." And in the morning he showed me, down by the water, the marks left by the helicopter skids, still in the sand. There were a few drops of blood, but what Lindsay remembered later was a young willow, no more than a branch, starting to straighten again after being bent sideways by the helicopter. Death and life co-exist everywhere, but it's easier to see in the Grand Canyon.

Those of us who seek nature sometimes want to be selective. We love the cold burst of rapids on warm days, but the day it hailed, we were less enthused. We want the rodeo ride down Hermit Rapid, but we don't want that same relentless current to be able to sweep a fishing man down the river. We want basic, elemental things like food cooked over coals and baths in the river, but we didn't sign on for the most elemental of all truths: Everything and everyone alive will at some moment cease to be so. We happened to be there for that final moment in the life of Todd Strickland.

We didn't know his name until later that evening. We didn't know he was a Tucson police officer. We heard he loved to fish and had a wife and two children. We wept, many of us. Some of those who had put their entire life force into trying to save him felt at moments that they had lost. They had achieved a pulse, had him warm and breathing again briefly. But then, Cindy said, it was as if he just left.

What I've come to believe is this: Our crew was not put there to save Todd Strickland's life. For reasons not clear from the underside of the tapestry, with all its knots and odd patterns, he was not to be brought back. I don't know his family, but I do know I would rather my brave and beloved father die in one of his favorite places than be needlessly gunned down by some punk with an attitude. I trust God more in the Canyon. Maybe because I'm less insulated from His world there.

The Park Service investigator told Dennis later, "He didn't die because of you guys; he had a chance of living because of you guys."

At one point, the prayer seemed not to have worked, but I've changed my mind on that. Todd Strickland might have died swallowed up in cold water; terrified and alone, thinking no one knew where he had gone. Instead, he was surrounded by people giving 100 percent of their physical and emotional selves to him, surrounding him with care and concern and tenderness. Maybe we couldn't pray him back to life, but maybe we could pray him to his next life, held and touched and wanted. I hope so.

After the sound of the departing chopper had dimmed, the boat had been unloaded, and the tents had been pulled out of protesting stickers and branches, we passed a flask of Irish Mist (a gift from a Vietnam veteran) and gathered around the fire. Circled in the dark, fortified by warmth, it's easier to talk. Cindy, who had said earlier she wasn't a spiritual person, belied those words by describing how the lights off the rotor blades seemed like a halo. Those who had been on the raft shared the story with the rest of us. Those who had been on the beach vowed none of us would walk out of camp alone the rest of the trip, and anyone near the water would be in a life jacket. We kept that promise; a legacy of Todd Strickland. I believe future river trips will have lives preserved because of him.

The next day we had to stop at Phantom Ranch, about 12 miles downriver from our camp. Drownings on the river shake up everyone whose work involves the Grand Canyon. Arizona Raft Adventures, our outfitter, connected Park Service interviewers to our group. Those involved wrote accounts; some answered questions.

We knew by now the Strickland family's story took up where ours left off. We knew there would be a funeral deserving of a 20-year veteran of the Tucson Police Department. We didn't know how to tell his wife and children, "He didn't go alone. We didn't know him, but we cared about him so much it hurt."

People bond in trenches. River groups always get close, but our ties go bone deep. I will never stop marveling at how Dennis could know a thousand quarter-mile stretches as well as he knew that one and respond so instantly to the cry for help. I admire Cynthia's toned biceps even more from having seen them pounding for a pulse, long after giving up would have made sense. Paul, Patti, Cindy, and Mike were heroes out on that emergency clinic on pontoons. They did the Lord's work. I stand in wonder of all of them.

None of that brings Todd Strickland back. But from the effort of the people, the beauty of the place, and the belief in the prayers, I think it wasn't meant to. He did not die alone. Those of us who were there will never forget him. People who were not there then will be safer in the Canyon because of him.

The next morning, I walked down to the river to splash off, and my first thought was to blame the water. But the Colorado isn't evil. It didn't do anything wrong. The result was tragic, but the process was as it should be. The river is still running.

I suspect Dennis and Cynthia worried about how the group would react to what we'd witnessed and done. Some could have wanted their mommies; complained the wilderness experience had been ruined; or simply been unable to coalesce what had happened. But we moved on.

We didn't forget Todd Strickland. We continued to talk about him through our last day in the Canyon. Yet we also savored our dinners, plunged into pools at the Havasu, and laughed when Lindsay or Paul or Matt made one of their matchless bon mots. We toasted our leaders the last night with admiration, respect, and love. Many lives have been affected by the Canyon. Sometimes, they end there.

Among those who love the Grand Canyon and make their lives in it, it is considered good fortune to die there. Like Bert Loper, slumped over his oars in a river rapid at age 80. Like others who have loved the river: agile photographers Emory and Ellsworth Kolb amd explorer John Wesley Powell. Like intrepid boatman Norm Neville who instructed rowers, "Face your danger!"

Todd Strickland is not gone. Just gone on ahead. As Edward Abbey wrote in *The Hidden Canyon — a River Journey*:

Night and day, the river flows. If time is the mind of space, the Colorado is the soul of the desert. Brave boatmen come, they go, they die, the voyage flows on forever. We are all canyoneers. We are all passengers on this little, living mossy ship, this delicate dory sailing round the sun that humans call the earth.

Joy, shipmates, joy!

chief yellowhorse lives on!

24 He may be gone, but his signs linger on.

Attention-getting because of the few billboards across the spare reservation land of northern Arizona, Chief Yellowhorse's red and yellow signs entice you coming toward Cameron, from the west or south.

"Buy From Friendly Indians," one urges. Then, in case you aren't sure how friendly, "Chief Yellowhorse Loves You." With a heart, like loving New York, or a dog on a bumper sticker. If you still aren't charmed and pass by the flag-fluttering stand off the roadway, you're begged to turn around after you passed: "Come back — You Missed Us!" and "Nice Indians Behind You." (My favorite, "We Take-um Master Card," must have blown over in the seemingly ceaseless wind that buffets you if you do get out of the car.)

Many years ago when I first stopped, it was to ask Chief Yellowhorse why he had a teepee erected out in front of one of his stands (yes, it's a chain of shops). How in tarnation, I wanted to know, is Native American awareness supposed to flourish if even a Navajo eschews hogans for the more recognizable shape of the Plains Indians dwellings? Just who exploit-um who here?

The "chief" genially answered that whites are always encouraging

Chief Yellowhorse's son Scott now runs the business.

125

self-determination by Indians and this was smart marketing on his part.

"Teepees go over better," he told me. "They say 'Indian' to tourists. Hogans do, too, but it's more subtle."

He added, "Built a teepee 65 feet high, once," not sounding like a man who feels ashamed of glossing over the details of his culture. "My brothers helped me. Took us all year."

Juan Yellowhorse got started in the tourist trade before he started losing baby teeth. His mother, who worked at the Petrified Forest National Park, would have him sitting outside in front of the visitors center to sell the Navajo rugs and runners she wove. These woolen works of art went for about a dollar. "My father made 50 cents a day polishing turquoise, so she did better than him," Yellowhorse pointed out.

Later on, his brothers followed him into the business. Sheesh was the last to join; it was originally Juan Yellowhorse and his brothers, John and Fred.

Wait — John?

The chief smiled.

"That confuses you whites," he said. "To you, 'Juan' is Mexican for 'John' in English. To Navajo, it's two names."

(I can just see the three partners in a business meeting — one rising and saying, "Hi, I'm Fred Yellowhorse, and this is my brother Juan and my other brother John.")

The next time I went to visit the chief, I took my father, and they discovered that, of only a few hundred people alive today, they shared memories of living near the New Mexico border around Lupton. They remembered Miller's Cave, now called Yellowhorse Cave since the chief purchased it, and the year the schoolhouse burned and classes were held in a boxcar donated by the railroad. They both had thought a girl named Betty was pretty good-looking.

Delighted with the shared past, Yellowhorse and my father exchanged a light correspondence, until two years ago, when my father's Christmas card generated a telephone call from the chief's son Scott, with the news his father had passed away in October.

But the signs, reassuringly, remain. When we go in, Scott Yellowhorse, the one who had called my father, is in charge of the operation, with his aide-de-camp Joe Cody, who was in residence the first time I stopped in to see the chief 13 years ago.

"My dad always wanted to be the McDonald's of the roadside," he says. "He got the colors from the old Whiting Brothers gas station signs."

Scott, however, is not "chief" now. The royals of Great Britain have it easy — your dad dies, you inherit the title. But Scott says his father began using the title "chief" after immersing himself in the ways and traditions of his people, the Towering House Clan.

"I don't think anybody could live up to what he's done in his life," Scott says earnestly. A lean man in his 30s, Scott could attract attention in much more crowded environs than this with his dark good looks and quiet confidence. But this remote enterprise is his calling.

Things look pretty much the same as they did before: Postcards and rugs and steer horns from Texas and Mexico share space with exquisitely crafted jewelry made by Navajo artisans, including members of the Yellowhorse family, still living on what Scott calls "the Reserve." After several mentions, I ask if this is what insiders call the reservation, instead of the Rez. No, it's just his habit.

"Reserve doesn't make it sound so . . . so . . . something, like you're rounded up. It's more like wildlife or nature that's protected," he says.

Scott hasn't changed the signs because, to him, this is the empire his father built, and the legacy is his to maintain.

"We kept the name in his honor. He was all over, into everything, always thinking about what to do next, where to go," he says. Surrounded by merchandise — in glass cases, hanging from rafters, and piled on tables — he reaches for a small, laminated photograph of his father, Juan Yellowhorse in a full war bonnet of feathers. I prefer another one near it, with the chief in the cowboy hat I remember.

"He used to say, 'Put your helmet on,' when we started to work," remembers Joe Cody. "Like we were going into battle."

Those were in the days when the stand was open-air, and every time the wind kicked up, Cody and the chief would have to scurry around holding down the whipping blankets so merchandise didn't go flying. This went on year-round, although Cody says it was worse in winter. "It would last some minutes. Or an hour. And cold."

It was all part of a campaign the chief tremendously enjoyed waging, chatting with tourists who still come through asking for him. Scott says gravely, "No one can fill his shoes."

But I'm not as sure of that. My daughter walks up with three cards brightly printed with information about tribes and America. Four dollars a card seems like a lot of money to her.

Scott smiles and begins to barter.

It's what his father would have done.

I know they buried the chief near Yellowhorse Cave. But I look up, wishing I could see Juan Yellowhorse watching his son and my daughter bargain. I believe he can and that he is enjoying it as much as I am.

Friendly Indians behind you, Scott Yellowhorse.

fire on the rim

25

The media dispatched news of the Rodeo-Chedeski Fire from this staging area.

Another forest fire. Because in 2002 the Rodeo-Chedeski Fire burned a half-million acres of northeastern Arizona, I'm more aware than I used to be when a new section of the state ignites. It's like one of those television screens that lets you watch a small image in the corner of a larger picture; right now, while my mind's main screen goes on with everyday routines, one corner has ponderosa pine trees crackling and falling under the rising specter of smoke.

The fact that my husband is at this fire, as he was at Rodeo-Chedeski,

129

may have something to do with my awareness. But he's been covering fires in KTVK-TV's satellite truck longer than I've known him. In fact, we used to cover them together when I worked there.

I rarely drive down the switchbacks into Oak Creek past Slide Rock without remembering a fire there in the early 1990s. We descended through layers of drifting gray, pungent with the tang of burning brush, into the thicker fog as we got closer. The visibility was so poor it was startling when an occasional boulder rolled down the slope to land by the road. It felt like one of scary scenes in a Disney movie; the dragon could be anywhere out there. Because the terrain is so steep, a few blazing branches sailed down, missing the car. As surreal as a parallel universe, Slide Rock was transformed from a sylvan sanctuary to an acrid underworld of ash and flame.

Which happened when the 1990 Dude Fire, along the Mogollon Rim near Payson, devoured Zane Grey's cabin and took the lives of several brave firefighters before it was through. (Nevada Barr described almost too well in her book *Firestorm* what it feels like to be a firefighter as the fire overtakes you, not just scorching but immolating the ground below, the plants around, and even the air you are trying to breathe.)

People living near Prescott never expected to lose their homes, but it happened the summer of 2002. And then the knockout punch was around Show Low, when two devastating forest fires merged and refused to be doused. Years of dreams, hard work, and memories exploded into white-hot oblivion as Rodeo-Chedeski roared through small forest communities.

My father told me years ago that the balance of nature did not mean stasis or neutrality. It includes tidal waves and huge fires, parching drought and saturating floods (this year at the same time in different parts of the world). The balance of nature has room for volcanoes, glaciers, soaking humidity, and sere alkaline deserts. That's as it should be, but it all worked a lot better before people got so ubiquitous.

Because nature's most spectacular views tend to be high-risk ones, we are drawn to the edge of the safety zone. The cliffs above California's beaches, where mudslides bring homes surfing down to ruin; Hawaii's lush landscape where lava spreads across the green. And Arizona's forests, where getaways seemed like a good idea until recently.

By clearing brush and trees from around forest homes, homeowners decrease the inherent risk. But a cabin surrounded by sheltering boughs is a cabin asking for trouble. Debate rages like the burns themselves: How much old-growth forest does it cost to thin the dog-hair thickets out? We have seen over time what types of forest management we don't want, but knowing in advance how to get the most safety with the least loss is tough. Never mind the politics and special interests that come with any decision so significant.

When my husband, Tom, and the television crews with him made the decision to remain in the fire camp after Show Low was evacuated, I spent some long nights picturing the worst-case scenario, which would be the subdivision across the street going up in a microburst of searing heat (they were already wearing masks against the falling ash during the day). I could imagine a rogue branch igniting something near enough to the satellite truck for the gas tank to go up in a whoosh; a fireball that would change my family's life forever. Part of me thought I was erring on the side of the melodramatic, but it was tempered by knowing that most of the homeless residents staying in Show Low didn't dream their lives would be altered this way, either.

To me, nature's least attractive attribute is the random selection process. You could be the person thrown out of the raft on the Colorado River; you could be the hiker struck by lightning on Mount Humphreys. Tornadoes don't do performance evaluations and decide to let the hardworking homeowners keep the fruits of their labors while just the feckless get whirled into oblivion.

And forest fires, which maintained balance in Arizona long before anyone drew a boundary and named it, burn through indiscriminately. Maybe if we lived in a poorer nation, where life is less protected and more uncertain, we would be more comfortable with the reminders that any control we feel is an illusion.

Outside Arizona's major cities, we live a little closer to the bone than people often realize. Hundreds of square miles of northeastern Arizona belong to Indian tribes, and on reservation land, the ratio of tribal police on duty to motorists on the roads is one you don't want to contemplate. If you had a heart attack, or a head-on collision, you could be a long way from help — especially if the air evacuation helicopter is busy somewhere else — even if you could get someone's attention. Dialing 9-1-1 works only when there's a cell phone tower nearby and a 9-1-1 system to connect to. There are landing strips in Arizona where planes have to circle several times before landing with critically injured patients, because animals graze on the runways between broken fences. We've "tamed" parts of Arizona. None can be truly, permanently conquered.

Fire is a fear dating back to childhood that, unlike most monsters, still has real teeth when you grow up. And it should. Respecting the tools nature wields is the only sensible way to co-exist with her mood swings. We are here not because we have conquered the earth, but because it lets us live. We can get evicted at any time. The fire doesn't care.

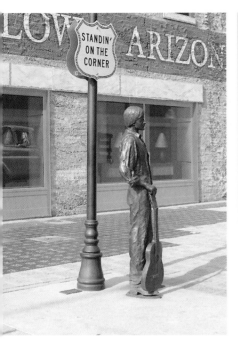

standin' on the corner

26

Actually, there are four street corners at the intersection in Winslow, as in the line from "Take It Easy," the Eagles' hit: "standin' on the corner/ in Winslow, Arizona." Three of the corners at Kinsley and Route 66 are decorated, if that's the right word, to evoke the sense of standin' on the corner. I guess it multiplies the photo ops.

The famous Winslow intersection includes these two views.

The most scenic of the three has a statue (perhaps of Eagles member Glenn Frey or just an archetype of the guy in the song?), a commemorative brick patio, and a truly gorgeous mural that looks . . . well,

133

like buildings on a street corner, but in more of an Edward Hopper landscape than standard-issue Winslow.

I've come to see the shrine with the other rock-music pilgrims, but I actually knew Winslow before the Eagles made it famous. My mother lived there as a girl, and our family visited every summer.

We're back now after a 10-year absence on my part. Driving up through Payson and Strawberry, my mother gets animated when we pull over the last hill that hid the expanse of flat, unlimited land — that red, bare reservation look says "home" to her.

Stories of her growing-up years have visuals: the little building that was Wild Horse Mary's brothel, where some friends got in trouble for putting up a red porchlight as a prank; her rather gorgeous high school, an impressive three-story edifice; the old Elks' Lodge where the Doonan Family Band played ("they also played the Arcadia Ballroom, the country club — if there was anything, the Doonans played there," she added).

And the corner itself! The Grand Café used to be on one corner, where she worked the breakfast shift; May's Jewelers on another, where her brother got his first job sweeping up; the Walgreen's Drug, where her boyfriend proposed in a back booth; and Central Drug, where the woman who ran the place always wore a hat. (Legend had it that her husband had always forbidden her to work, so after he died and she sought employment, she wore the hat to maintain the appearance of being just another shopper.)

We drive down the streets that my mother remembers cruising in her brother Paul's lovingly rebuilt Model A, a group of friends all singing in harmonies as they rode. (That reminds her of the night some cutup "borrowed" the town hearse, to make the ride more interesting.)

First stop is La Posada, the historic hotel which is gradually coming back to the splendor my mother remembers as a little girl. Of all the buildings architect Mary Colter designed for the Fred Harvey Company in the early part of the 20th century, this was her pride and joy; when she heard it was closing, she said, "There is such a thing as having lived too long." Built to resemble a land-grant scion's hacienda, it's a custard-colored adobe with tile and long verandas.

We go into the lobby, and Mum points out the phone booth, carved out of a medieval drawbridge gate.

"The bellman stand was next to it, and I would pretend to make calls so I could see if the cute bellman was there," she says. She shows me the former banquet room, where she would have liked to have had the wedding reception at her and my father's wedding. But it was too expensive: "Dinner would have been a dollar a person."

So our lunch today could have fed 20 wedding guests then. We sit in the restored dining room, sipping hot tea and looking at the stained glass of St. Pascual, who Colter included in the design because he was the patron saint of hospitality. Replete, we wander the halls, reading names of celebrities who stayed here in its heyday, including presidents and movie stars. (Although wouldn't Clark Gable and Carole Lombard have shared a room?) The wood is deeply polished, the sunken garden still boasts the fountain made of a massive piece of petrified wood. High Mission-style benches and round chairs make inviting seating vignettes throughout. Mum remembers coming when it was the Santa Fe train station to pick up relatives, and even getting to play the grand piano in the lobby, although a different piano stands there now. We are charmed and leave hoping La Posada can attract the crowds it deserves and needs.

'Cause it's pretty clear, back in the car and driving around, the rest of the town ain't gonna do it.

We love Winslow, my mother and I — we drive past what used to be Ross' Drug where we both enjoyed limeade at what her brother Paul called "the eatin' counter." She points out a tiny building that was "the second hospital, when the first one got too small." We drive past her old house, with the screened porch and the silverlace vine covering the chain-link fence.

But other than that, Winslow is a town where stasis has turned into decline; along many streets, a well-kept house stands out, and many businesses supply basic needs but not indulgences. I hope that its proximity to Flagstaff, where property values have soared, will make Winslow an attractive bedroom community in a few years. We agree we could sell our homes in Phoenix and Tucson and get a palatial abode here.

Years ago, I was talking to Tommy Thompson, who then ran the Winslow Chamber of Commerce. He explained his plan to rename what had become Second Street to Route 66. The Mother Road, which had been bypassed by Interstate 40, deserved some attention, and Thompson believed the familiar black and white signs would generate enthusiastic tourists.

"What else is black and white?" he asked. "The space shuttle! If they put a Route 66 sign on the tail before they flew again, Route 66 could stretch from Winslow all the way to the moon! Well, you know what? I wrote NASA! And . . . they haven't said no!"

His enthusiasm was heartening. I have thought many times since, waiting for news that could be good or bad, "They haven't said no."

Winslow, with its midwestern neighborhoods, porches, and sidewalks, is a town on hold. The population has grown slightly in the past decade, according to the man behind the counter at the Route 66 store. But there is something dejected about much of it — empty sidewalks, boarded buildings. It is a stage set, waiting for the troupe to discover it. The world hasn't said no to Winslow, but it hasn't said yes either. I hope it does.

on the arizona trail

27

Dale Shewalter first conceived of the Arizona Trail sitting on Coronado Peak watching the moon rise.

"I was feeling the significance of the place," he said, "with the passage of the first Europeans into what is Arizona today. And I thought, if there could be a trail the length of Arizona, it should start here."

Hikers who walk through this trailhead marker at Oracle step into history.

"Here" was where, in 1540, Francisco Vasquez de Coronado made the Spanish La Entrada with his expedition of explorers into what became the United States. Four and a half centuries later, Shewalter's dream

137

became reality with the dedication in 1988 of the first 7 miles of a 790-mile trail linking Arizona's northern and southern borders — with a heaping helping of scenery in between.

Seven mountain ranges, five lakes, four rivers, three national parks — no golden rings, but the Arizona Trail does afford unlimited majesty and magic for those who feel the open road luring them to travel some section of it.

Before the trail's dedication, photographer Jim Randall and I got to travel with Shewalter to shoot a half-hour documentary about the Arizona Trail for Tucson's KGUN-TV. It remains the best piece I ever did for television. We began where Coronado crossed into what now is Arizona. Shewalter, with his handlebar moustache and booted stride, could have been a Rough Rider or frontier explorer if he'd been born sooner. As it is, he did plenty of rough riding and exploring when he mapped how the trail would link existing paths to form a cohesive course.

The Arizona Trail passes Parker Canyon Lake, which calls people who like to take their nature straight and pure, without much company, and without competition for some of the best fishing in Arizona. It goes over the Santa Rita Mountains into Sonoita, where we met two young women on a packing trip.

Kate Beardsley and Kiyo Taylor had taken a semester off from Prescott College to help survey the trail. Learning to manage pack horses and taking notes of trail and water conditions gave them a challenge they felt worthwhile. Randall's footage captured their determination and energy as they crossed a golden field with their animals, helping give birth to the Trail.

Up past Tucson, over Mount Lemmon, the Arizona Trail descends next to Cody Ranch. We met Dean Pritchard, who said he had loved owning this ranch near where he was raised.

"I felt both joyous and guilty," confessed the rangy University of Arizona professor, "because it should be shared, this area. Then I heard about the Arizona Trail and found out it would come through here."

Pritchard fixed up the corral that sits next to the trailhead arch at the foot of Mount Lemmon near Oracle.

"Man and horse have operated on trails for 80,000 years," Pritchard said. "It's one huge last chance for people to partake of something we've always done: be in touch with the land."

Up through copper-mining country, the Arizona Trail passes Apache Leap. Legend says this is where warriors leapt to their death to avoid capture, and their women, watching, wept what hardened into the shiny black stones known as Apache Tears. Near Superior, the trail travels fossilized wagon tracks left by early settlers and mining trains.

I remember Shewalter describing the mid-state transition zone, where layers of mountains fall away like veils in the distance: "Picture the Mogollon Rim dancing with the desert."

The East Verde River is another water crossing, where the river's constant caress has polished rocks smooth and cool. It isn't deep and offers a staging area for horses and hikers.

From here, the Arizona Trail passes Mormon Lake and goes into Flagstaff. Flagstaff has long boasted an urban trail system using the Rio de Flag, which seamlessly accommodates the Arizona Trail. We went during a snowstorm, and watched an eagle make its graceful patrol over the area, before we headed on to the Grand Canyon.

Because if the Arizona Trail is to be the Southwest's answer to the Pacific Crest or Appalachian trails, it must traverse the Canyon. This is far and away the most traveled section of the Arizona Trail, where tourists walk the Bright Angel Trail to watch the Canyon, with sun and shadow dancing in its depths. Some of nature's finest work is on display here, created by her artists, water, wind, and time. The Grand Canyon calls to some as the sea does with a constant awareness of its existence and a longing to return.

The Arizona Trail's terminus is smack dab at the state line with Utah, in House Rock Valley. When the desert varnish was just faint swaths of color on the Paria Cliffs, tribes lived scattered over this area. Shewalter was concerned about ruins being preserved.

Back then, talking to us, he was hoping the trail would be complete by the year 2000. It's not far off schedule, for a venture that includes state and federal agencies and a wagonload of logistics. The Arizona Trail is for people who want to answer the call to come and see; who know that finishing isn't the best part.

Sitting around a campfire the last night of our time with Shewalter, I remembered John Wesley Powell writing of sharing a similar night with the small band of loyal boatmen who rowed his wild voyage down the Colorado River. Enveloped in darkness broken only by the flickering flames, Powell described a feeling of camaraderie and timelessness "so sweet it is almost a grief."

I remember the time on the Arizona Trail that way. Meals and jokes shared, something to drink at the end of the day to take the rough out of the road; connecting with others who knew the restless urge to take in as many miles, as many vistas and visits, as possible. No one can repeat another's experience on the Arizona Trail; weather, pace, and company are integral ingredients of the trip. But for every person intrigued by the idea, the one promise the Arizona Trail holds is that memories will be forged in its steps.

traces of ed abbey

28

Edward Abbey watched for fires from this tower along a road marked by crooked aspen.

We walk down this dusty track near the North Rim of the Grand Canyon on something of a pilgrimage. We want to see the lookout tower where ecology writer/activist Edward Abbey once worked as a fire watcher, a time he refered to in various writings. Even as I trudge, I am dimly aware that Abbey himself would probably scorn a person for seeking out a relict of someone else's experience with nature: "Go out and have your own!" he might say. But I have heard of the "crooked forest" of aspen on this rutted road, and now I am in it.

Like other legends, Abbey continues to grow years after his death in 1989. Patron saint of eco-terrorists and ardent environmentalists, Abbey was a classic example of someone who longed to comfort the afflicted and afflict the comfortable. Writing about Abbey is somewhat like writing about the Grand Canyon: You know it's been done, and it will be difficult to do without drawing on "awesome, vast, grand." Yet, because he casts a shadow as long as the fire tower he climbed, I have come to look.

The Forest Service advises against climbing the tower now; too tilted to be safe. But again I'm aware Abbey would despise my blind obedience to authority. Mocking someone in uniform was one of his hobbies. "Climb it if you want!" he would say. Ed Abbey isn't really my kind of person in many ways: Often awful to women, he glorified drinking too much and didn't really think there were two sides to issues if he felt passionately about them. But as a writer, there is so much to admire.

In his early journals, before he wrote for an audience, is an "Inventory of the Self" done at age 25, or "one third dead," as he put it:

"I've been loved by people whose lives I value almost as much as my own . . . have written one-fourth of a magnificent novel . . . afterwards, eight more, even greater!

"I want to see an earthquake or a tidal wave. I want to spend a few weeks in prison. I want to blow up St. Peter's.

"In everything that's happened to me, I've found something worth chewing on."

Then he bursts into the kind of poetic excess that sent electricity through his work, describing what "like jewels on purple velvet, have been the great moments of my life; the first time I heard a great symphony and thought the world must end."

Abbey's mother greatly influenced him. Her own journal shows what both nature and nurture gave "Little Ned." She wrote, "Who said there is no perpetual motion machine! The Atlantic is exactly that — roaring and rolling, plunging and tossing."

Jack Loeffler, a longtime friend of Abbey's, once described him as tremendously curious, adding, "he spurred me to thoughts I might not have had otherwise."

I think that's the greatest tribute a writer can receive: to tap a well-spring of insight and discovery in a reader, rather than just handing down pre-digested wisdom. Read Abbey going on a tear about something, or someone, and your mind can spin, throwing off comet's tails of huge thoughts and concepts he introduces. Abbey needs to be chewed in small bites.

Abbey never aspired to be put on a pedestal; he was much more comfortable down in the dust and grit and guano of the desert floor, where he found the poetry and majesty of life. Reading about him, one gets a sense of a flawed, contradictory, emotionally careless man, both inspired and blatantly human. People do not idolize Abbey because he was perfect, but because he reminds them of themselves: passionate but practically powerless. Abbey's real call was to seize the smattering of power each person can scratch together and do something freeing and creative with it, not because you have earned the proper credentials, but because you don't need them.

Next to the fire tower is the small cabin that Abbey occupied. I peer in, feeling silly because on one level I know there won't be any leftover journals, or even tomato cans, giving me fresh insights into the man. But at the same time it's interesting to know that this was wood upon which he walked. This was a porch from which he observed the sky and the trees. This birdsong, this dust, this diffused sun, was familiar to him. It's like getting to try on his coat.

At the same time he cultivated his iconoclastic reputation, Abbey was a voice in the wilderness wanting to be joined by a chorus. The man who pointed out there was a difference between civilization and progress didn't have to worry about what would happen if the wilderness got crowded with people fighting for its preservation. He knew well that profit and nature are too often mutually exclusive.

Abbeys' friends and followers have always warned against making too much of the man. Doug Peacock, the model for Abbeys' famous character Hayduke, who inspired the phrase "monkey-wrenching" by fictionally sabotaging bulldozers, once said he tended to avoid events honoring Abbey because the best way to pay tribute to him was to skip something Ed himself would have thumbed his nose at.

Author Charles Bowden, the closest to being given the Abbey mantle, pointed out that Abbey did his thesis on anarchy. He was not a get-along guy.

Leo Banks, another talented Western writer, is sanguine about Abbey's legacy because of his personal relationships. He finds it hard to stand in wonder of someone who was often so lousy at human interaction. (Abbey might well have agreed; he may have belonged to the "I'm not a role model" camp of Charles Barkley.)

I wish I could report that as I was contemplating Abbey's worth and contributions, standing in the shadow of his former fire tower, a vulture circled overhead and cawed raucously — Abbey had hoped to be reincarnated as a vulture. But none did. No words were whispered in the rustle of pine branches. Nothing mystic happened. That's actually exactly what Abbey would want to have happen: *For cryin' out loud, you go mooning around thinking about someone else's footsteps, instead of taking your own journey, then you deserve to hear silence.*

And hearing that silence, soak it up, take it home, for the days when you are constantly surrounded by noise. Guard your time alone in nature jealously. Better yet, do whatever the hell you want. That's walking Abbey's road.

the certainty of being disbelieved

29

Percival Lowell's
mausoleum rests
atop Mars Hill.
The Pluto Walk
displays
information
about the
planets.

Lowell Observatory is one of those rare places where the present echoes the past. If you want to take a snapshot at Boston's Old North Church today, you have to frame it carefully to avoid including any traffic with the old building. No one is cleaning a long rifle where Davy Crockett stood at the Alamo. I hear the Holy Land provides a real challenge for pilgrims wanting to immerse themselves in the New Testament experience. But at Lowell, you can not only see the telescope used to discover Pluto, our ninth planet — the telescope is still in use.

Up in Flagstaff, the clear nights are spent scanning the skies, searching the stars, to find out more about galaxies far, far away. That much of it is done from inside a control room, in front of computer screens, shows the once-removed condition of many human occupations. Pilots used to have to look at the skies instead of at instruments; doctors had to watch their hands instead of monitors. Bartenders used to have to know how long to pour an exact ounce, instead of using a dispensing gun that measures amounts. An astronomer once told me that sometimes he walked out on the catwalk around the big telescope just to reconnect himself to the larger picture.

Lowell Observatory sits on Mars Hill. It's not named Pluto Hill, because while Percival Lowell's assistant, Clyde Tombaugh, did discover the far-flung orbiting iceball from there in 1930, Lowell himself devoted much of his life study to the red planet of Mars. Convinced that the lined images he observed were canals, he burned to be able to prove conclusively that sophisticated life had inhabited Mars at some point.

When Lowell was working, Flagstaff was even less challenged by light leak than it is now. To be out with the rustle of pine- and sweet-scented breezes while the city slept must have set new standards for work environment. Lowell, and men like him, watched.

The best illustration of the planets' relation to one another is the Pluto Walk at Lowell, models of planets the proper size and distance on a small scale. Tombaugh's achievement at the telescope is mighty: After a cluster of planets close to the sun, Pluto is both small, obscure, and a long, long way up the walk.

Few things constructed by man are as mystic and classic as the telescope dome. Turning, seeking, it is slightly of another world, majestic. Like a tall ship under full sail, the telescope can connect us to vast mysterious places. Standing out in a light mist of rain under a sprinkling of stars, it's easy to see how, for centuries, we have responded to the mystic allure of the sky at night.

Astronomy is a passive science. Chemists can mix elements; physicists can set up experiments. But in the world of science, astronomers are the romantic cousins. They are journalists of the solar system. They can only observe, interpret, and report.

This third step — reporting — stirred Lowell to pen what is to me maybe the most eloquent prose on any memorial. His mausoleum, on the edge of Mars Hill overlooking the city, provides him with a resting place that's almost heaven in itself. Designed in a simple echo of the classic observatory dome, it uses shaded glass and granite as a lasting monument in a quiet garden. On the sides, two of Lowell's writings are engraved. The one that moves me refers to his study of Mars and his own hopeful hunch that he would be able to bring data down from the mount showing once and for all that there had been Martians tilling the furrowed fields he was sure he watched through his long cold nights at the eyepiece.

"Astronomy now demands bodily abstraction of its devotee . . . to see into the beyond requires purity . . . and the securing of it makes him perforce a hermit from his kind . . . he must abandon cities and forego plains . . . only in places raised above and aloof from men can he profitable pursue his search . . . he must learn to wait upon his opportunities and then no less to wait for mankind's acceptance of his results . . . for in common with most explorers he will encounter on his return that final penalty of penetration, the certainty at first of being disbelieved."

A venerable journalist named Bert Sass told me once that it is almost impossible to be judged on the merits of our efforts. Depending on factors beyond our control, the path we pursue either pans out or deadends. The result, which is generally hard to know on the front end, "either makes us a hero, or a goat," he said. A merciless public has been with us always: Politicians, scientists, writers have been reviled through time for coming up with something a little too against the party line. But far outside the box is where the greatest discoveries lie.

When I was a television reporter in Tucson, I did a story about a man sure his holiday song about a black reindeer was destined to join the realm of classic Christmas music. We went to interview him, and in the smoky living room of his leaning mobile home, he told us how country music stars had been approached and were considering recording his beloved tune for release. He sipped from a highball glass lifted between tremors. After we left, Clyde Kirkpatrick, the photographer, paused before returning the video camera to its case.

"There is nothing as noble, or as sad," he said, "as a man's dream."

I hope that at the end of his life Lowell didn't regret the years spent chasing a vision that turned out to be just that. I hope he didn't think tilting at windmills a foolish pursuit. His Martian oasis turned out be a mirage, but he had no way of knowing that going in.

A ninth planet is a fine thing, and I'm proud Arizona is one of only eight places in the world where one of earth's siblings was discovered. But the true value of Lowell Observatory is the monument to Lowell's dogged pursuit of something that turned out not to be. To his willingness to go out on an astral limb for a possibility. For one man's dream. A man strong enough to "forsake the plains" and endure "the certainty of being disbelieved."

monsoon over miami

30 To experience Arizona, you must witness one of its monsoons. That's the widely accepted name for the late summer thunderstorms that residents speak of with the reverence some use for Olympic opening ceremonies or the aurora borealis.

The overture for this symphony of storm is a breeze, rustling and snapping branches as its intensity grows. Now become a ruthless wind, it evicts rattling tumbleweeds and dusty underbrush from the desert. The temperature can drop 15 degrees in 15 minutes, although if you watch the

A summer storm bruises and streaks the Arizona sky.

149

thermometer on the fence, you miss the advancing army of dramatic clouds.

The wind just gives the bugle call heralding the arrival everyone's been waiting for. Over the mountains, or just sweeping across open sky, the troops come as one: thick heavy thunderheads, charcoal gray and ready with their relentless arsenal of rain.

You hear the monsoon as well, first in the engine rumble of far-off thunder, followed almost immediately by a bright after-image of the sky having cracked open directly above you, with a boom that rattles the windows and startles even the most experienced storm-watcher. Then, the thrumming of rain, that might start gradually like beans pouring into a pot, or could as easily break open like a piñata, drops slapping big as pancakes on the hot pavement. And the scent! Part creosote, part wet dusty asphalt, part paradise, it's a siren smell that anyone who has breathed of deeply wants to breathe again.

All day you've dragged like a lizard in the heat, slouching through the torpor and humidity in a sweaty shirt, glancing overhead now and then to see if you can pick up an early warning sign of the monsoon. But it doesn't give early warnings. It charges and attacks.

You stand looking out at the tempest that has transformed the city you know into a German opera of sound and movement, stirred to restlessness. Eucalyptus branches toss like dizzy giraffes; established trees seem bent at geometrically impossible angles. (Often, they are. Driving around after one of what my grandma used to call gully washers, you see trunks and branches scattered across roadways and lawns like a sloppy giant's toys.) Monsoons are not nurturing. They hurl rain like an assault, so fast the desert can scarcely begin to absorb it, and then move on, leaving streaming curbside rivers of mud-brown water for children to skip, slip, and shriek through once the storm has passed.

You may venture out while it's still raining, to feel the battering breezes and the fat raindrops on your arms. (Or maybe to roll up the car windows) You may stay inside, wishing you were part of the maelstrom of lightning and downpour.

If you're driving when it hits, you probably wonder if it's true that rubber tires protect you from lightning strikes. Searing bright branches of electricity play keep-away, taunting from every direction. Sometimes, by trying to count, you know it's dangling just over your head — a high-voltage tickle waiting to descend. Drivers around you are dim red brake lights while the pounding on the roof drowns out the radio. But if drivers wanted to open their windows, they'd probably be pumping their fists and whooping rather than complaining. This is what we live for during the days of that euphemistic "dry heat."

Every summer, some foolishly optimistic motorist underestimates the speed and force of the running washes and ends up having to be rescued from a dip in the road or a downtown underpass. Water here is such a foreign visitor that many people don't understand the language. If you've seen even video of a flash flood, or a wash filling with runoff, you know the power of the summer rains.

The Diné, also known as the Navajo, refer to female and male rain. Female rain gently soaks and renews the earth as a misty rain that adds to aquifers and lakes. Male rain comes as the monsoon: abrupt, impolite, overwhelming.

While normally the desert is largely brown (we should have as many words for brown in Arizona as there are for snow in Alaska), monsoons bring out the color. A type of ruellia bush wisely closes brown seed pods over bare stems until soaked by rain, and then the pods open and begin shooting seeds in all directions, recognizing that right now the ground will be briefly moist and receptive to new life. Nature is canny. Leaves turn green faces upward. The next morning, the desert will be soft shades of sage, olive, fern, along with the usual cinnamon, cumin, and nutmeg.

Half the annual rainfall comes during these bursts that roil down the empty riverbeds and drag debris across low ground. These storms define us, in their independence and thoroughness. A monsoon pulls no punches, plays no favorites. It is an all-inclusive baptism, a resplendent excess of the water of life. And we drink it.

the man who talked to ravens

31

Even though I haven't seen Jim Norton at the rudder of the *Raven* for almost 20 years, he's still there in my mind, guiding his raft of recruits down the Colorado River.

Norton was the reluctant BRG (Bronze River God) who piloted the first two raft trips I took through the Grand Canyon. He made almost as big an impression as the river itself.

We wondered how this big-bearded bear of a man somehow managed to make animals see him as brother rather than threat; how a father raven would slowly walk up to meet him on a strip of beach and take bites of pancake out of Jim's hand, to carry back to his brood. How a wasp would share his morning cup of coffee, balanced on the opposite rim of his huge rusty mug in the drop of honey Jim carefully poured for that purpose.

This was a man who walked on rocks so he would leave no footprints to mar the landscape; who would answer mildly "Your guess is as good as mine" to theories others might have laughed at. He was that respectful. Of all life, not just human.

He introduced us to his view of the world, which was that every aspect of nature deserved equal consideration. When my brother Lyle

Jim Norton pilots the *Raven* on the Colorado River.

153

was stung by the most dangerous type of scorpion, Jim scooped it up and carried it gently to the water's edge. It was only trying to survive. Cradled in the web of his logic, we didn't protest. It all made sense at the time.

My journal entries from the trips bring back the river that was Jim Norton's natural habitat as surely as it was the raven's:

"Thunder promised but didn't deliver last night; sheathed like a forlorn and bewildered mummy, I listened to wind whip the groundcloth while I scrutinized the clouds."

"Jim just told us the story of Bert Loper, slumped dead over his oars at age 80. If I get to die doing something I love that much, fantastic!"

For a city girl, I saw the side hikes as journeys of more than just distance. They offered a look at a world I couldn't have dreamed into being: the stark, dark, surreal walls of Saddle Canyon, with the thin silvery streak of water weaving down to a nest of pale ferns; the ghostly imprints of nautiloids fossilized in ancient rock. And of course, the river itself, from 40-degree slaps of rapid waves to the brilliant turquoise baths at Havasu Falls.

It began to dawn on me that, with a finite number of elements in the world, all water is related. The surging Colorado River is kin to raindrops, which are distant relatives to the water in Tucscon's swimming pools and the fountains in downtown Phoenix.

"It poured today, dripping from grey sponge clouds into the tall black otherworldliness of the Inner Gorge," I wrote.

Nothing captures your focus better than terror. Traversing the rapids, I developed a sense of water's potential force.

"Jim said Crystal may be the worst rapid on the river. We swirled so close to the rough rocky sides! Indifferent waves dash against the Canyon walls; boats can too, for all the river cares. Crystal loomed like a funeral where you aren't sure who died; a mammoth hook of muddy water, a can opener to the morass of dervish waves."

And what that same water hath wrought! The Canyon looks even more incredible from the bottom, gazing up at the cavalcade of carved sandstone and shadow.

"Limestone intrusions here; the wildest buckles and folds in the rock! I can almost hear what it must have sounded like pushing its way through, hounded by a volcanic eruption, seeping and splitting the rock. Now, millions of years later, we see pale ribbons crisscrossing the cliffs like ethereal graffiti."

With his physical calm, gentle voice, and huge laugh, Jim Norton introduced us to all these things — and formed 17 disparate personalities into a temporary tribe. His lessons included his unexpected reaction when the motor sputtered and died — just before we swirled off the liquid lip into a bucking rapid. Discovering the previous crew had not replaced the spare motor, Jim threw back his head and laughed.

"Just when you think people have surprised you every way they could, they find a new one!" he said. I remember that response when I'm dealing with a crabby clerk, too far from the Canyon for comfort.

I don't know where Jim Norton is now. I know he did a variety of things since I last saw him at Diamond Creek, soberly waving goodbye as we rattled up the dirt road in a rickety bus.

But I know where the Colorado River is. It's being wasted. It's coursing through carrot peels in my sink, condemned to trickle into sludge and sand before reaching the ocean. We are both thirsty. But is it carelessness, or cruelty, to render such a powerful river impotent before its goal, like netting salmon just feet from the spawning ground?

Lavish lakes and subsidized crops are part of the problem, but it is not enough to say, "I won't change till the big guys do." Watering the street as well as the lawn, letting the shower run during what was supposed to be a short phone call, rinsing the sink while finding and sorting the peaches to be washed — all are violations of the spirit of water in Arizona: It is scarce and sacred and should be treated as such.

So every time I take a shorter shower, or turn off the tap while scrounging for a pan, I'm honoring Jim Norton's legacy.

If I could figure a way to send every Arizonan down the Canyon along the Colorado River, it would be the most powerful water conservation incentive possible. Once you've seen the water in its roiling glory running Lava Falls, water that we now will let casually gush from our faucets, you don't want to treat it lightly any more.

AUGUST

straddling the colorado

32

It isn't easy to come home from vacation.

Work waits for you. All the petty problems you put aside are hovering over the house when you return. All the things you packed so neatly before departing are now tumbled and dirty.

Like about a third of all Arizonans, we head to California every summer. When I was a child, it was to visit grandparents or Mickey Mouse. As an adult, I take my children to see my brother Lindsay in Long Beach. The traditions are magic: the swimming pool, the Crab Pot restaurant

A Long Beach marina harbors pleasure craft.

157

for sourdough bread, the pool again, the statue of Slick the Seal on the pier, the pool, Lindsay presiding over his famous grill. And the pool.

While Arizona is heaven to me, crossing over the Colorado River to come home feels like ferrying across the River Styx at the entrance to Hell. Because we always go during the hottest part of the year — the heat being the whole reason for the California escape in the first place — Arizona doesn't have much to recommend it. You get out of the car, in whatever border town you choose, and a blast of superheated wind hits your legs. Between going through the mail that's stacked up while we were gone and longing to be back at the dockside restaurant basking in the breeze, I've had to dig down for what makes me sure I would never move one state over:

The air. Our skies spread as a landscape all their own. The huge, slowly rolling clouds of blinding white that build into towering thunderheads crawling over Flagstaff's San Francisco Peaks, the wisps of gray virga from a faraway storm fringing over the desert, and for dessert, the sunset. Gathering like a full cast for a final ovation, any and all clouds are transformed into sublimely rich shades of coral, gold, and purple. Arizona's finest art, each sunset is gloriously unique. But while your eyes cling to the last shifting shades of swiftly muting hues, remember that another show opens at sunrise.

California skies, on the other hand, are as salty, fetid, and dull gray as an old sweat sock. There is no dimension overhead nor any sense of soaring to the edge of the atmosphere. The coastal sky hovers just above you, faintly brackish. It's also humid. You may appreciate being back home from vacation most when you step out of your shower and grab a towel so dry it crackles. In southern California, there are only degrees of wet, from "wringing" to "damp." Here, your hair will be dry before you button your shirt, instead of still faintly moist when you go to bed.

All the fancy talk in the world won't change the fact that we don't have the ocean. Okay, I've said it. Arizonans love nature and need to hear the beating pulse of the earth in the waves. That immersion in the water that has the same percentage of salt as our own blood is reason enough for Interstate 10 to exist. But between visits, we do have water in some pretty amazing forms. Oak Creek, waltzing and reeling down the rocks in Sedona, richly scented with moss and sun-baked rock. The wide open invitation that is Lake Powell, with its vaunted miles of shoreline. And remember that Californians may have the Pacific, but they have to come to Arizona for the highest, fastest navigable rapid on the American continent: Lava Falls in the Grand Canyon.

We don't have theme parks like Out There, but the hooked and twisted snag of a dying ponderosa pine against a stormy sky rivals any witch on a Snow White ride. The crowd at the Grand Canyon is as multicultural as "It's A Small World." We don't have pirates singing and swinging tankards, but I'm not complaining. And it's possible that at one of those roadhouses up north . . .

Many of us shop while we're in California, which is where I notice the best part of living in Arizona: the people. The sourdough starter of Arizona's population is not very cohesive. It's filled with iconoclasts from somewhere else who each brought their particular brand of independence with them.

When I was in California, I was aware I didn't see a single female wearing her hair as I do. (California brings out an exaggerated awareness of physical appearance.) It seems there is one standard for beauty in California, and everyone is somewhere below it on the scale. Here, there are as many ways to be beautiful as there are races and cultures mixed up together, and natural state is not something to be fled.

In southern California, towns blend together, marked merely as exits on freeway signs. Here, you can travel the state and hear accents that vary from place to place: the rich twang of Camp Verde, the covered clipped tones of the Diné on the Navajo Nation, the melange of Spanish and English in border towns.

Diversity is a dry word, but it's a great feeling.

I'm not saying California isn't worth a trip. Signs that say "Beach

Cities" and "Slip Renters Only" are a nice change from "Watch for Deer" (or elk) and "Do Not Enter When Flooded."

If life were made of either/or choices, there wouldn't be law libraries. Father Kino was kinder than Father Serra, but the missions Serra established have lasted better. They have Yosemite. We have the Grand Canyon. They have the smog, we have the heat.

It's not a matter of one being better overall. It's which whispers your name; where you are most truly among your own. It's your bones recognizing something longitude and latitude can label, but not explain.

We go. We enjoy. We wisely come home.

wind over wupatki

33

Maybe it's off the beaten path now, but Wupatki was once in the midst of things.

The ruins of dwellings dating from the 1200s sit on a loop drive north of Flagstaff; they share a national monument designation with Sunset Crater. (This is a bonus, with the glossy, twisted, alien lava fields you pass. No matter what you do, a photograph of the tumultuous crust seems to turn out in black and white.) Coming from the north, which is how we always seem to approach, you wind past smaller ruins before

Wupatki's ruins show the builders' flair for sturdy, distinctive architecture.

161

you reach the visitors center. Any one of them is worth seeing, especially if there are no other cars parked there.

You can see ruins regardless; to see through the veil of what's concrete and what's perceived, it's best to be alone. The dwellings of ingeniously stacked rock stand on high ground, and the view in every direction is the sere scrubby grassland, garnished with some low juniper. Hundreds of people lived scattered over this site, and many of the ruins are still unexcavated. It's odd, when driving in, that you don't see the ruins from miles away. There is just enough hill and dale to obscure the main site from view as you meander along the road (the first one that we've seen that uses painted cattle guards instead of installing metal bars).

Wupatki, which means "tall house" in Hopi, is my favorite Arizona ruin. It's true that Tuzigoot in the Verde Valley has the most amazing collection of cosmetic and decorative items, and at Homolovi just north of Winslow, I got to see ancient leftover parched corn still cached in one room. But Wupatki's windswept citadel holds a special place in my imagination. Perhaps the fact that the view seems unchanged since Wupatki's time strengthens the sense of actual people having lived here.

In its heyday, Wupatki was a linchpin in the trade routes of wandering tribes, with New Mexico's Chaco Canyon to the east, Montezuma Castle and Casa Grande to the south, Walnut Canyon somewhat west, and Canyon de Chelly to the north. Relics show that here traders exchanged copper bells and parrots from Mexico and beyond, Pacific Ocean shells, and all manner of beaded goods. It was a commerce center, a mall, a place where information was distributed. and relationships renewed.

When you wander the path starting at the visitors center, again you can savor it best in solitude. A few times, I have arrived just before closing to enjoy the hush of early evening, when time seems to hang suspended before swinging from day to night.

Without seeing the roofs, it's hard to know how the rooms were sectioned off: one per family (and if so, did some include a loft?), or several in a row? We know most activities took place outdoors. I find striking where someone interspersed the rock work with decorative borders. I imagine it was the women, somehow, who made it important to add the round rock layers between the long flat sandstone ones. I listen to the breeze, hoping somewhere in the wind lingers an echo of voices that murmured and sang here.

Its stone glowing rust and russet against the sometimes impossibly blue skies of northern Arizona, Wupatki is visually stunning from many angles. Especially at sunset, of course, as the shadows lengthen and the coral and bronze burnish the walls. Visitors are allowed to enter a room and see from the inside out. A bulwark, a fortress, a landmark, Wupatki lets you see for miles.

Because Sunset Crater's volcano had exploded mere decades before the area was settled, layering the ground with mineral-rich ash, the farming is said to have been easy and abundant. So on these plazas, women ground corn, prepared beans and squash, visited. The children surely romped across the ball court when there wasn't a scheduled game. And dogs probably led and followed the hunting parties across the long stretch of land toward the San Francisco Peaks.

If you follow the path to the far end, you reach Wupatki's crowning glory, the blowhole. A natural system of underground caves and tunnels conspire with air pressure so that a whoosh of air is always either coming up or rushing down. What did the residents made of this? Was it a god, a voice, a trick? Did it signal favor or ill will, depending on the direction? Or did they, as wise in this as in many other things, recognize that the air pressure had changed? Sitting by the blowhole, feeling that constant steady cool breeze flow up and out, is like getting a telegram from middle earth. It is timeless and mysterious and surely forges a link with the residents who did the same thing centuries ago.

I used to wonder how people could fully experience something without language to assign to it: "humiliating, elegant, whimsical," would need words, wouldn't they? But on a hike in the Inner Gorge of the Grand

Canyon, I experienced a heightened alertness to every rock, breeze and scent and realized, as I picked my way down, that I wasn't thinking in words at all. I was immersed in awareness, not needing a vocabulary.

So I don't wonder if the architects of Wupatki had words for bronze, sienna, and auburn to describe the colors shading their stonework. They stood here. They saw this. They were part of the landscape and the process of altering it in a way I can only wistfully imagine.

If I were given a chance to travel back in time, I might even forego some of the classic moments in history and choose instead to stand at Wupatki, looking off down the long straight pale path, watching traders moving slowly toward my home. Then I would walk down to the blow-hole and listen to what people said about it. The best I can do, now, is be there at dusk and watch the colors grow more intense on the straight stacked sandstone, trying to peer toward the past.

a woman's place

34

In all Arizona, this is to me the most powerful place.

Here at the foot of the Vermilion Cliffs, I feel more awed, more alive, than anywhere within the boundaries that arbitrarily define this state.

One of my brothers once saw a movie he said told lots of different stories: King Arthur, the sword in the stone, Camelot, Merlin the wizard, the Holy Grail. As underisively as it was possible for a teenage sister to do, I explained that those are all truly part of a larger legend.

To me, Vermilion Cliffs country is that way: the phantasmagoric

The root cellar shielded Emma Lee and her children from the heat.

165

rock sculptures, the ribboned colors of the cliff walls, the walk into the Colorado River, the looming span of Navajo Bridge, the red dust and willows —all in the same place.

The first time I saw Lonely Dell, it was because our boatman on a Colorado River trip, wanting to put some space between us and other departing rafts, took us on a hike rather than sit waiting at Lee's Ferry. Since then, each time I've returned, I've been more reverently intrigued.

If you ask, "What Is Lonely Dell?" I can give you the short answer: the homestead where John D. Lee and his wife, Emma, lived while operating the ferry across the Colorado River.

They came in 1872, and she lived here for seven years. Much of that time Emma managed without John: first, because he traveled for the fledgling Church of Jesus Christ of Latter-day Saints and to visit his other wives; later, because he was in prison. (When he was legally executed in Mountain Meadows, Utah — shot so as to fall into his own coffin — for his role in killing innocent pioneers there, it's fairly well agreed that he took a fall for church leaders. Some Mormon officials had encouraged wiping out outsiders who might have become too comfortable and stayed in what was seen as Mormon refuge. But that's a tale of another place.)

Lonely Dell was where Emma wrote her letters to her husband in jail and single-handedly raised a family, ran a farm, dealt with traveling strangers, and kept the ferry going. Second-shift working women existed long before the term was coined. They just never clocked out or got paid.

John D. erected the buildings and established the ferry, but it was Emma who lived here. You feel her presence looking at the fruit trees she tried to keep alive by hauling buckets of water when floods washed out the irrigation system; her steps you imagine at the low root cellar door, where her children avoided the brutal summer heat. The Forest Service now tends the orchard of peaches, plums, pears, and apricots, but when it was just Emma's buckets to do the job, all but one apricot tree died. The gardens and outbuildings stand as a pinprick of rustic gentility under the raw, wild majesty of Vermilion Cliffs, and the contrast enhances both.

Birdsong and dust filter through the dry air as I approach, and I feel the way I would entering a cathedral, a place that brings out our loftiest selves and comforts our deepest weaknesses. At Lonely Dell, two log buildings with stick-and-willow roofs housed the Lee family, or Emma's branch, anyway. John D. had six other wives. In the cabin, now called the shop, Emma gave birth twice. Frances Dell was born just after Emma moved in, and "Dellie" was almost 2 when John was away and Emma sent the children outside so she could deliver Victoria alone.

No record exists, but we know the bright soothing tones we would use to our children, telling them Mama will be busy awhile and it's very important that they play well together. How we would set our lips against crying out and frightening them! Without pills or ice or clean cool sheets, without any soothing words or hands, how bitterly alone she must have felt tying off the umbilical cord. Did she cry into the new baby's soft skin? As shadows over the mountains provide the depth to them, sorrow is the grace note that makes Lonely Dell so compelling.

Walking up from the breathtaking delta of Lee's Ferry, I see Lonely Dell as a pocket of green tucked under the Vermilion Cliffs like a baby bird under its mother's wing. It's an oft-told story that upon arriving, Emma exclaimed, "Oh, what a lonely dell!" and her husband promptly proclaimed the spot as named. John D. spent the next two years shuttling between there and a nearby wife Rachel's home before being arrested. Earlier, when John had surveyed the site with Jacob Hamblin, he had written that "no woman would take to such a place." But, at the only Colorado River crossing until below the Grand Canyon, Mormon settlers coming from Utah to rural Arizona Territory needed the ferry service, and Emma wasn't asked how she felt about running it. Sometimes with help, often just with the eldest son, Billy, Emma rose to the job.

It's too bad Emma Lee didn't sense a comforting destiny brushing her skirts when she served breakfast to John Wesley Powell's team on their 1872 return mission to the Grand Canyon. Or know that her bravery would be documented when she faced a group of unfriendly Indians by bringing her children and their bedding down to the Indian camp and sleeping there as a show of trust. The chief, impressed, moved on and repeated the story.

I came to Lee's Ferry pregnant once, and jogging up the road to the cemetery, I began to feel ungainly. But, thinking about Emma tucking her children into blankets in the hostile camp, the feeling vanished. This was not a place where women were remarkable for soft hands or a pretty dress. This place measures femininity in strength, not fragility.

Even my father thinks Lonely Dell is a woman's place. On one trip, he said he didn't think he would have liked John D. much if they'd met. This surprised me, because John chose to die rather than fink on anyone else involved in the massacre. Wasn't that brave and noble?

Brave, stupid, my father shrugs. In his mind there's nothing noble associated with walking into the house three days after your wife gave birth in that low dark room. Nothing strong about riding off to go exploring with the guys, leaving your woman and small children at the mercy of heat, flood, raiders, disease, and bone-crunching work.

John D. Lee earned the name Yawgatts from some local Indians, which means "Man with Tender Heart." Emma loved him fiercely enough to walk away from the gentler elements of civilization before she set up Lonely Dell. His picture shows a face belligerent, strong, maybe reckless. But although this place bears his name, to me it is a monument to a woman. It seems a place to be reminded that women, too, were pioneers, even though their bravery didn't always lie in battling rapids or Indians. Their daily courage came in continuing to put out breakfast for children without worrying out loud about whether their father was returning, or even alive; carrying water to the last little tree after the rest withered because it wasn't in them to quit; planting and washing and nursing and teaching and singing in an alien place because this is where the husband pronounced home.

As stirring as the Vermilion Cliffs are, they are just the setting. Lonely Dell is the story, a story not often told: of unwavering bravery on the part of women who may have been loved by men, but couldn't be protected from life's worst by them.

summer's gone

SEPTEMBER

35

We have just more than 12 hours of sun today.

Since summer solstice, I have checked daily the newspaper's weather page for the scheduled time of sunrise and sunset. For a while, it was an embarrassment of riches: The two were more than 14 hours apart. But that splendid surplus is over, and we're in a slow slide that's closing down our daylight rapidly.

This shortening, this quickening, makes me nostalgic. It makes me evaluate the year, far more than the artificial ending date of New Year's

Turning trees on Northern Arizona University's campus proclaim autumn's arrival.

Eve. The year is ending now. Nature, the true calendar keeper, is winding down.

I hang on, looking backwards, like a kid pulling away from Disneyland would watch through the station wagon's back window until the freeway ramps finally block the Matterhorn from view.

And yet, that same kid might find himself, somewhere past the Denny's restaurant in Yuma, starting to anticipate seeing all the guys at school again. It's sad to see vacation end, but it's exciting as well. It's fall.

I remember walking with Dale Shewalter, founder of the Arizona Trail, this time of year. We tramped the wonderful 2 miles of scenery around Buffalo Park in Flagstaff. He pointed out that the sunflowers were pretty well gone and that the chirp of crickets was rapid. Once he mentioned it, I remembered the lazy languorous cheerrriipppp of long summer nights and realized they were speeding up.

That accelerating, that briskness, carries across all nature, as if the pulse of the earth itself is ramping up. It's the final burst of energy kicking in at the end of a long run, using up the little left in a spurt of excess.

I've started most of my new jobs in the fall, as if the old school calendar is genetically inhaled. After the ease of summer, industry is actually appealing again. Activity sounds interesting instead of too much effort. Organize those photos. This year we will buy that cord of wood. It's as if it's taken me the first two seasons of the year to figure out how to drive the thing, and now I want to get in some miles before curfew.

We've passed through the unsure potential of spring and the sultry star-drunk stretch of summer. The seasons of new growth and life are gone; we're in the final lap. Nature may be losing power, but she'll burn up the engines in a full-throttle, all-boosters, fireworks finale.

So we get red leaves.

The woodbine is starting to rustle toffee brown and rich burgundy instead of fresh green. Pretty soon aspen will be doing that incomparable aspen thing. "As gold as . . ." doesn't do it. Clear, almost neon in its purity, aspen is the gold standard, if you will — the shade by which all others should be measured.

In some parts of our state, fall is subtle. Southern Arizona gets what my parents dubbed the "chinook," a stir of early morning breeze in August that gets more sure of itself around the time school resumes. No more beach towels on the line, it whispers. In Phoenix, I see the change in the now-empty blue pool where I usually do laps. Swimming is out of vogue. Helen Hunt Jackson's poem about "October's bright blue weather" was probably written in a cooler clime, but the sky turns from merely pale to something closer to actual blue in the cities, and its color absolutely gobsmacks your eyes up in the high country.

We seem excited by the change; winter fashions appeal again, even though the temperature hasn't dipped even close to chilliness. Christmas-tree permit applications have been available at the Forest Service ranger station since just after Labor Day. Elk hunters are in full court press, firewood collectors head out and enjoy the very different sweat of working hard in cool weather.

But there's nostalgia as well. In *The Great Gatsby*, Jay Gatsby strolls down to his elegant swimming pool at the end of the summer. A few leaves drift across the water's surface; there is an abandoned, elegiac feeling to his final swim. It captures the transition time: a loss of interest in all things hot and decadent, and an awareness that the ripeness will soon turn into decay.

Winter will come dark, slow, deep, soft. Cold (to some degree). Autumn is the glory of full potential, of harvesting full fields bare. Autumn realizes it's the one with the bounty, the experience. It's like the rich confident resonance of a woman's voice once she's in her 40s and finally realizes she's fascinating. Autumn is the surge of a football kickoff, a relay race on a new playground. It's also the poignant moment spent looking at a harvest moon, feeling the year turned as burnished as the gold.

We come home, move closer to our families. We want to lay in provisions, stock, collect, plan. We're rushing about now so we will be ready to settle in.

Fall is preparation and also a pause in the music — a rest between movements in the symphony of seasons that gives emphasis and attention to what both comes before and follows after that hanging hush. Fall is when we realize that what begins must also end, so that it will be able to start again.

Bring it on. And mark its passing.

un, river, run

36

When it rains, they run.

Arizona's rivers and washes soar to life after a rainstorm like someone's added water to concentrated crystals to create mega-mondo floods. Not just water casually filling the dry washes and low, dusty riverbeds. Not just runoff seeking larger tributaries. This is surging, unleashed water with an attitude — water with a fist planning a breakout.

I'm standing with my brother Lyle in his Tucson driveway looking over the bank of the Rillito River. I used to live two doors down, the

With an angry surge that can't be dammed, Oak Creek breaks over its banks.

173

only place where I've ever bought flood insurance. For four years I watched the rising sun's rays crawl across the riverbed that was dry in practice, even though its job description was to carry snowmelt and rainwater. The term "river" in Arizona is largely a ceremonial position. But after two raging days of rain last week, it was running double-time, bank to bank.

I've never seen it like this: rolling branches, whisking trees, hurling propane cans and other looted booty in its path, shaving off slices of land as it roars around the curve. It's grabbing earth and shouting — a waterway on a rampage.

Lyle and I, more accustomed to the bland beige sand behind the retaining wall, are spellbound: nature has created a monster in the wash. We aren't alone — neighbors wander out with umbrellas and video cameras. We shout to one another, partly to be heard over the sound of churning water, partly because we're excited.

"Looks like the Mississippi!" yells a bearded man whose two sons are looking longingly over the wall. I agree with him and sympathize with them. I, too, hear the siren song of the water daring us to find out what we're made of. Could we stay afloat in that current? What would it be like in that stampede of deep brown waves? It reminds me of the Colorado River. I've rafted it several times, and this river seems to be moving just as swiftly, and with as much disregard for anything human-related.

It stirs our blood. Lyle and I linger by the wall, almost dizzy from watching the undulating standing waves by the opposite bank. Suddenly we hear a rumble. The hungry runoff has devoured another section of earth. Earlier we'd seen a power pole pulled in. A string of stables are folding, farther down.

The man whose property is being repossessed by the river stands on the bank. I don't want him to think we're feeding off his misery as if the destruction is just theater. I cup my hands and yell, "We're so sorry!" He waves. He looks tired.

It's raining hard again. Lyle has to go to work. I drive back to my parents' house with my baby, feeling skittish. The proverbial fire horse, I've seen waves I can't raft; I'm wild to explore other bridges, see what other damage the anarchist, nature, has done.

I leave my napping daughter with my mother and race back up to the Rillito. A sinkhole is forming on the jogging path that I've run for years. What I know is altered; this is a parallel universe, where Tucson is flooded. A storm makeover.

From the Swan Road bridge, I look down. The Rillito beckons me down the steep bank over the barbed wire. Attraction and fear; what would it be like to be carried on that teeming tide? Would I be snagged on that passing fence torn from some riverside pasture, now beating against the bridge support?

Water does this to people in Arizona. Its rare appearance galvanizes us. When we have it, we have it in spades.

I hear Oak Creek has slipped its banks and washed out the park of Los Abrigados Resort. I remember touring the area when the resort first opened in 1986. My father, who grew up in Sedona, looked at the picnic tables and manicured grass and said, "All this will be washed away sometime." I couldn't picture the docile creek turning so ferocious. But I am not the one who remembers hollering across this same creek when other bridges have been swept downstream. Now, the bridge I walked across to get married is gone, and debris is 4 feet high in the trees we stood beneath. I'm sorry to hear about the loss of that landscape, but I'm impressed with Oak Creek's power. I'm reminded that we are not in charge. Nature permits us to live here, like a management company permits changes on the property. But the true owner can — and does — come in and put things back the way she intends for them to be. Our landscaped lawns are a privilege, not a right, that rain has revoked.

We hear about the Little Colorado River seeping beyond its boundaries and flooding Bushman Acres in Winslow, which was "the part of Winslow where you'd want to live," my mother, a former resident, says. Not now — its custom colors are all sienna floodwater. People assumed that where the water was, the water would stay. They didn't really comprehend that all land within a large area around any riverbed can be annexed by a flood. Rains like these shake up the status quo, and cost a lot of money, but they also remind us that nature is not a wimp. The natural order prevails. Humans are tenants, not rulers.

Water in Arizona is like the northern lights: brief, dazzling, powerful, and more meaningful because of its rarity. We bring our camcorders and lean on the rough wall, for a moment able to watch the earth back in charge of itself, carving new angles in the banks and changing what we will see when we look out our windows of the homes we think are forever.

Sedona and T.C. Schnebly pose in 1900, the year before they pioneered Oak Creek Canyon.

he woman behind the name

37 In the century since the town of Sedona was named after my great-grand-mother, Sedona Schnebly has been transformed from an obscure settler from Missouri to something of an icon.

The name captures some indefinable Western exoticism that makes it attractive to manufacturers of everything from salsa to furniture; it's odd, still, to see it in ads for such things.

Occasionally, it borders on disrespectful, when someone writes glibly of how the original Sedona would enjoy a margarita and a massage at an

Oak Creek resort if she were to visit today. Sedona Schnebly had a work ethic of iron, and none of her grandchildren ever saw her relax past the point of visiting with a neighbor while she embroidered.

But any public figure, living or dead, is open season in modern marketing. All I can do is try to portray her correctly for posterity.

Which is its own problem. Could you portray yourself for posterity in a thousand words? What would be interesting to others? What would you rather everyone forget? How do you sum up the you that was an adolescent, a college student, a young spouse, a parent, and beyond?

I can lay out Sedona's bare biographical facts, as relating to Arizona, in a single sentence: In 1901, she came from Gorin, Missouri, with her husband T.C. Schnebly, whose brother had urged them to move to the exquisite canyon in the West he had found.

The couple built the first two-story house in the area around Oak Creek Canyon, and with T.C.'s trips to Flagstaff selling their crops, they became a bed-and-breakfast of sorts. I was told by the grandson of one of the original settlers that when people got off the train in Flagstaff and indicated an interest in seeing Oak Creek, they would be directed to go to Babbitt's store and find out when Mr. Schnebly was due to arrive. Bringing passengers and supplies led T.C. to apply for a post office license, and when Schnebly Station and Oak Creek Crossing were pronounced too long to fit in that little stamped cancellation circle with "Arizona Territory," the aforementioned brother suggested naming it Sedona.

Even when I was young, Sedona the town was not much more significant than, say, Winslow or Williams. Artists have always been drawn as bees to honey, but in the 1960s, merchants were still known to refuse service to hippies. And when Sedona Schnebly died in 1953, she was mourned as a good friend and neighbor, but not as a figurehead. That has come since.

So what's worth recording? That Sedona grew up in "the second-most prosperous family in Gorin" (I guess in small towns, it's easy to keep track of these things) and learned several foreign languages as a girl. Gently bred, she and her siblings nonetheless had plain rooms and plenty of chores. Her distinctive, deep-set gaze shows in early photos, and someone remembers her being referred to in girlhood as "that little bug-eyed Donie Miller." (Growing up, I hoped that was a typographical spelling of "big-eyed," but I doubt it now.)

She met and married T.C. (Theodore Carlton, but he signed T.C.) at the same time her sister, Lily, was being courted by Loring Johnson. Because T.C. had the unfortunate distinction of being Methodist in a Presbyterian town, the scuttlebutt was that "Phillip Miller was getting 100 sons-in-law: Loring is one, and T.C. is double zeroes."

This may have had something to do with the newlyweds' decision to migrate west. Still, a well-deserved thump on the head to those town gossips, as T.C. immortalized his wife by naming arguably one of the most beautiful places on earth after her, and Loring ended up in Leavenworth Prison for embezzling.

Sedona liked blue. She had long, dark hair, which T.C. liked to watch her brush, saying it had "nature's own permanent wave." She sometimes wore overalls working around the farm. We don't know what her wedding dress looked like, which strikes me as sad since getting married was such a pivotal event in a woman's life in her time. We have a photograph of Sedona, in a hat like a floral wheel, sitting in the back of a Model T on her way to a Temperance Society Conference in St. Louis. So we know she gave up a lot in terms of modern conveniences to bring her two small children to wood-floored tents while their frontier house was constructed.

An itinerate reporter's account for an Eastern paper reports taking Thanksgiving dinner with the Schneblys and lists, among other items on the menu, a large hollow squash stuffed with cabbage and seasonings. So Sedona had at least a touch of entertaining flair.

We know the saddest chapter of her life was the day her 5-year-old daughter, Pearl, was killed — Pearl's cow pony bolted during roundup and she hadn't been holding the reins. Sedona went into such a decline that the doctor told T.C. he must move his wife or risk losing her. They returned to Missouri to make peace with the family and then went to Colorado for some years.

Sedona's daughter Clara recalls her playing the organ on rainy days and making the children march in time through the rooms of the house for exercise. She describes her mother singing as she worked and getting ruffled if someone walking with her wasn't in step. So we know she had idiosyncrasies.

Another daughter, Genevieve, died of cancer as a young mother of five. A son-in-law remembers Sedona up in the middle of the night with several of those children, rocking them and crooning lullabies in German until they slept. She embroidered everything that held still, included her long white nightgowns, which were "2 inches below the floor." She must have hated cold feet.

My father remembers his grandmother as being "more Martha than Mary" — providing, nourishing, teaching, but not playing or teasing much. He also remembers her tirelessly drilling him on Bible verses.

If I were to choose one defining fact I know about her, it is her friend Ruth Jordan's memory of the night before Sedona died of cancer.

"There was a terrible thunderstorm," Ruth recalled. "I heard a knock at the door, and there was T.C., drenched to the skin. He had a get-well card for my father-in-law. He said Sedona had heard he wasn't feeling well, and nothing would do but for T.C. to bring the card down right away."

To be that close to death and yet send someone else a get-well card is as other-centered as I could ever aspire to be. She may or may not have felt the energy of the vortexes; we don't know if she danced among the red rocks. But we know she willingly lived in the service of others. That's a worthy legacy.

When I speak at schools about Sedona, I tell the students that when she was their age, she would have had no reason to believe anyone would ever want to know about her life. She left no journals. The closest I can get to her is to walk down to the creek where she did her laundry and try to picture her there on the bank, which is now part of Los Abrigados Resort, and see what she saw (some of the same trees, I know.)

Then I say that, someday, we all will be ancestors, either through our children or those of relatives, and someday someone may be very interested in us.

So write things down. Maybe no one will name a town after you, but your great-grandchild may be as curious about you as I am about my forebears. A journal from any one of them would be priceless beyond measure. It doesn't have to be a novel. A page, or a paragraph, would be more than I have from Sedona.

Run off a few emails you've sent. Print out a letter you've saved in a correspondence file. Stick a note in your Bible. If we can learn from the past, it is to record the present. For in the future, someone will find it fascinating.

hart prairie wedding

38

Photographs won't show how cold it is. Elise and Rob will be forever captured in the twilight of the golden hour, radiant and newly married, on the deck over the slopes of Flagstaff's San Francisco Peaks at Hart Prairie Lodge. The chilly temperature will be invisible.

If we, as guests, have scanned the skies all day, first under grim clouds, then through sleet, later in rain, we know how even more anxiously the bride has witnessed today's changes in weather. "Well, this if Flagstaff!" we say, with helpless shrugs. It has snowed here on Memorial Day and then not again until after Christmas. Anything is meteorologically possible. Elise knew this; she has lived here for years. But she and Rob are outdoor people, and outdoors the wedding must be. In town, we shake our heads and feel sad for her.

But as we drive from Flagstaff to the Arizona Snowbowl turnoff, the rain stays behind. Blue skies and bright sunshine (thin, but visible) bathe the lodge's flower-garlanded deck. The wind makes it cold, but it is clear, and for now, that is enough.

A duo plays classical selections, even though the wind keeps tugging at their sheet music. The round rims of portable heaters don't offer much warmth, but we huddle there anyway. The women who drove up

Newly married and radiant, Elise and Rob Wilson refuse to acknowledge the cold.

from Phoenix in open shoes and sheer sleeves are starting to huddle in husbands' suit jackets.

Behind me, waiting for things to get going, our friend Jim sits alone. His wife died a few years ago. I wonder how many weddings he has witnessed since then. Anyone who has outlived a spouse, or survived a divorce, does not go to weddings the same way single or married people do. There is an element of opportunity lost, destiny missed, for the divorced or widowed. Bittersweet or mocking or poignant — it depends on how the marriage was, and how it ended.

I know this partly because of Jack Penland. Going to the first wedding he attended after his wife died, I made him take me as company. His wife had been young when cancer claimed her. I knew seeing the bridal white, the happy couple, would be superimposed for him with visions of the glad groom he had been with her. So I told him we would go together, thinking that at least being in the presence of someone who would acknowledge the difficulty would help.

Like this, it was an outdoor wedding. Like always, watching the bride come slowly forward toward her new life, I think of Jack's words.

"Weddings are a lot like funerals," he said that day, "and baptisms, for that matter."

"Because someone presides, and we all dress up and sit in rows?" I asked.

"That, too. But mostly, they're all about hope," Jack said. "We know the divorce rate is 50 percent. We know how hard it is to be married. But when we come to a wedding, we let ourselves hope that for this couple, life will be gentler than for some.

"And we know how hard it is to grow up. We know about drugs, and peer pressure, and thinking your parents are hopelessly wrong in every way. But at a baptism, we put that aside to hope for this baby, that those little feet won't have too hard a path to walk; that the innocence can stay, for at least a while.

"Then, at a funeral, we're hoping again. Even those of us who say we believe in heaven don't know for sure. All we can actually see is the hole in the ground, or the urn, or the absence. So again, we hope that we will see this person we loved, someday. We gather, to hope."

Elise and Rob are saying their vows. Elise resisted love until she was in her 30s, and she finally abandoned her reservations in the face of Rob's unswerving sureness, after he drove nonstop from Flagstaff to Denver and back to pick her up where she was stranded, and afraid to fly, after September 11.

People in their 30s don't see marriage the same way younger brides and grooms do, either. For those in their 20s, it's still an adventure, this concept of a new life together. Like a cruise, presumed to be all dancing and brunches and leisure. Now the adventure is more like a whitewater trip — it will probably be very uncomfortable at times, and if someone gets hurt, it could turn very bad, very quickly.

Because they realize this, Rob and Elise say their vows with a certain resolve you don't know you're going to need when you're younger. Her voice breaks — this day is undoing a lot of old hurts and beliefs. And when they turn to face the guests, Elise is glowing like the sunlight behind her. She may have been afraid, but she has not let her fear make her refuse the adventure.

Afterwards, there is the dancing, and there are the toasts, and the deep loyalty and approval of her brother's words make some of us cry. When I step outside, the sky is so bathed in stars, it seems to be another world. What a perfect place to begin a marriage, in the clear cold air, above and away from the pollution and noise and human-caused distractions cities invariably carry.

I have attended weddings that seemed like a bad idea — "They should just sign the marriage license and the annulment with carbons at the same time," someone once joked. I have — thankfully — been to weddings that seemed doomed and yet are still happy marriages two decades later. Jack was right; life is unknowable before the fact.

"If we ever knew what we were getting into," one of my brothers once said, "we would never have the courage to do anything."

Elise and Rob will take a honeymoon. They will open all the gifts stacked on the table. They will sober, sometimes, at what it means to join two lives. But they will have the photographs that captured the way they looked tonight, smiling bright as the sky, out on the wood platform, with the Peaks and the pines and the breezes witnessing that what God hath joined, let no man put asunder. And the rest of us, seeing them together, can feel very comfortable in our hope, that for them, the sun will always come out just at the time they need it most.

teacher, teacher

39

The historic schoolhouse in Strawberry brings to mind the appearance of a remarkably youthful older woman.

For its age, the Strawberry Schoolhouse remains a remarkably well-preserved feature of its little community northwest of Payson below the Mogollon Rim. Walking around the old building, noting its picturesque outhouse's half-moon door, I find myself thinking what I sometimes do about a remarkably youthful older woman: "I think some work has been done here."

A sign at the site makes the careful distinction that the Strawberry Schoolhouse is *believed* to be Arizona's oldest wooden schoolhouse. It

187

doesn't say so, but I'm guessing that qualified statement is a nod to the Hopi village of Old Oraibi, the oldest continuously inhabited settlement in Arizona and possibly the nation.

I've come to see the schoolhouse as a gesture of homage to Arizona teachers. Just down the road in Payson, the Julia Randall School is named for a beloved educator who taught several generations of early settlers' families. There should be a register here at the Strawberry School, for visitors to write messages about the teachers never forgotten. Too often, I doubt the teachers have any idea.

My grandfather, Ellsworth Schnebly, taught in one-room schools like Strawberry's most of his life. He wisely declined offers to move up the educational ladder, or to larger districts. Chambers, Mayer, Parks, Dinnehotso, Fredonia, all hosted him throughout his long career. Even after retirement, he finished a term at Beaver Creek School, back in one room. Besides standard subjects, he taught mythology, classics, and lots and lots of good values. His influence bled through to my father — I have finally learned that it's easier to go for the dictionary to look up a word I don't know, than to live with the vague unease I feel just skipping over it, dropping the educational ball.

Our high school English teacher may not remember saying, "With all leisure and no work, leisure becomes work," but I have thought of it many times since. Dathel Lackey radiated such passion for Shakespeare some students found it amusing, but then were drawn in by her zeal. Now in her 80s, she still has more sparkle and energy than many of her former students, 40 years younger. Because it's almost impossible to limit the process of teaching to solely the subject, Mrs. Lackey also set an example of what a difference enthusiasm made, how women can be very professional and still nurturing, and the value of memorization. (I was very glad to be able to tell her this recently, as well as reciting Portia's speech from Julius Caesar, which I memorized my junior year.)

Sometimes the legacy spreads beyond the students. I didn't have

Sister Domitilla, but she taught my mother's third-grade class that just because you are done with sin, sin may not be done with you. I've recalled that often, ruefully.

If our lives are shaped by those who love us, and those who refuse to love us, the strict teachers deserve credit. My freshman English teacher, who ran the school newspaper, denied me a slot on the staff, saying I lacked the qualities a journalist would need. I wonder how much of my years in newspaper, television, radio, and magazine journalism have been spent working to prove him wrong.

My mother teaches that if even one person believes in a child, that child has a chance to make something good in the world. I think that one person is often a teacher. Lew Losoncy, a motivational speaker, told of being the scourge of his Catholic schools until a nun took him aside and said he was the only student who was able to drive the sisters to profanity, "and if you can make a nun cuss, you have a real power."

My first-grade teacher honored students periodically by having one stand in front of the classroom while the rest of us sang "I'll Take You Home Again, Kathleen," substituting the honoree's name. The story feels absurd in its telling, but I've never known the same flushed pride I felt in front of that chalkboard being serenaded by 6-year-olds.

I don't know where Mrs. Quay is now. I never told Mrs. Lewis that when I hear anyone used "everyone" and "their" together, I think: "The singular antecedent 'everyone' requires the singular, masculine pronoun 'he,' because the gender is unknown." Our teachers live forever in our brains.

Mr. Sobecki doesn't know that I got permission for my child to check out a library book every day, just as he once let me, because it did so much for my perception of myself as a reader. (He also mocked my use of "teensy-weensy," instead of "microscopic," when describing plankton, making me realize I wanted to go into a more fluid and descriptive field than science.)

From a child's point of view, I couldn't have told you in grade school which teachers would remain with me. As a parent, though, I can see the seeds being sown with my two children.

Mr. Pantera offers his students the universe: radio plays, Shakespeare, "pi-ku" poetry (each successive line of verse has the same syllable count as the value of pi as it progresses), the art museum, Latin lessons, even recording a blues song they wrote. More than that, he demonstrates a passionate curiosity about the world that shows them they will be happiest continuing to learn their whole lives long.

If there were a register of appreciation at the Strawberry School, we could flip through and get a sense of all the teachers who were willing to stand up in front of an often indifferent class and put their hearts into teaching. Those willing to be laughed at, like my third-grade teacher when she fell down playing dodgeball, and my fourth-grade teacher every time she dyed her hair. For being willing to be scared, probably, like an eighth-grade teacher who was told a student's big brother was going to come after her.

We can't pay them enough (although we could try a little harder than we do now) for the value they give. We cannot always find them later to tell them how much they meant. But we should start a guest book, so others could read about the significance they had in our lives.

My first college boyfriend, a military veteran passionate about societal ills and determined to change them, went into real estate instead. But a few years ago, he became a teacher at Picacho Elementary.

"Remember," asked William Ferguson, "how I always said I would change the world? Well, now I can — one child at a time."

I think he's onto something.

spooks along the highway

40

On Halloween, residents along Senator Highway in Prescott welcome the things that go bump in the night: children.

Trick-or-treaters all, hordes of costumed enthusiasts jostle for space along the sidewalks, curbs, and sidestreets of what is technically Mount Vernon Street, an older neighborhood graced by Victorian homes and cottages. A tradition for decades, Halloween along Senator Highway is not for the faint-hearted — or frugal — resident.

"Last year, we gave out 3,000 packages of candy," Michelle Sensing

OCTOBER

A Prescott home welcomes trick-or-treaters with Halloween decorations.

tells me. "And we didn't stop because they stopped coming; we ran out of candy."

They come on foot, in cars, in red wagons. With their dogs, who get a special doggy treat from a different bowl. They even come on buses, from as far away as Phoenix. "Youth groups, churches, classes, and just people who like the tradition," says Sensing.

She and her husband, Mark Caldwell, are more than ready. Spider webs adorn ledges and light fixtures. Realistic ravens encircle one cloudy hemisphere of webs. An immobile butler offers a tray of Reese's peanut butter cups with a frozen flourish. Orange lights mark a runway from the wrought iron garden gate to the porch.

I first came here on Halloween in the 1990s to do a story for KTVK-TV news about the trick-or-treaters that descend on Halloween. The Sensing family welcomed my photographer and me into their traditional gathering, where friends and family enjoy soup and sandwiches while distributing treats and admiring the costumes, from whimsical to pageant. At the time, Isabelle was a tiny toddling lion in a furry mane. Now she is an elegant column of a goddess in a peacock headdress, distributing candy. Molly is the wee person in residence, fetching but twitchy in her organza witch's dress.

Michelle's family bought this home in the mid-1980s, and she says the Halloween pilgrimage (if we can forgive the mixed holiday metaphor) grows every year. It's easy to see why; residents may know that this is the street in Arizona with the most homes in the National Register of Historic Places, but the rest of us are drawn to it for less technical reasons.

We like the varieties of the past we see here and of the places — the Midwest, neighborhoods in Boston and upstate New York — hinted at as we drive under the changing colored trees and scuff through real fall leaves. The gables and arches and pillars and balconies on the bungalows and mansions and Craftsman-style cottages captivate us.

Halloween decorations are a lagniappe, the extra bit of something that Creole merchants traditionally included in a customer's package.

Now with elaborate autumnal trimmings over the spindled porches, grinning pumpkins lined up across the railings, it is a splendid vision.

A single perfect rose is one kind of beauty — a whole field of tulips is another. Halloween here is of the latter variety; the sheer volume of costume and decoration overwhelm. If one man on a unicycle wearing a gold crown and doing tricks is interesting, a hundred of the same would be so much more so. And to be part of the teeming crowd is like trying to move down Wall Street; swallowed up in the masses, you are both hindered and protected by the tide of humanity surrounding you. You are a straw in the bundle, a drop in the puddle, a part of the whole.

Things start early. The sun is barely setting when the first visitors arrive. These are the younger set, chubby and soft and looking slightly confused as they solemnly extend their buckets and bags for candy and compliments. The parents stand back with the strollers; some stride up, confident they have earned the treats as well in their Valkyrie braids or hatcheted forehead.

The next wave is the family groups where older siblings can supervise the blinking toddlers through whispering "thank you." Now you see more bleeding masks, warriors, and sultry vampiresses. The waning hours belong to the teens, who have crossed beyond the age boundary for traditional trick-or-treating, and would be given the disdainful look candy-givers save for those they deem too old. By 9 o'clock, all but the determined or thoughtless have vanished back into the darkness from whence they came. We've enjoyed the revelry and decoration of Mardi Gras without the debauchery and decadence.

Vandalism isn't a huge problem, Sensing says; it's too crowded for anyone to pull something without being seen by dozens of people. She worries more about the dangers of traffic; residents of Senator Highway have been trying to get the street closed, or at least an alternative route established, to cut down on cars.

"There are 8,000 to 10,000 a day now," she says. "You can't sit on your porch and have a conversation." Without a crosswalk for school children, or the option of shutting down the major arterial route on Halloween, Sensing worries that it is a matter of time before the price paid for inaction is too high. Some families are so concerned, they have stopped participating in the tradition.

It would be sad to see it go; sadder still, obviously, for tragedy to put an end to the ritual. But most of America's beloved customs have survived hard times, from champagne toasts during Prohibition to presents under the tree during the Depression.

Senator Highway strings along a prized collection of homes that have managed to survive termites and demolition to be restored and carefully improved upon. If there is any place where spectacle and ritual can survive, one would hope it would be among the ornate and beloved homes here, which have themselves prevailed over the ravages of apathy and time.

she never checked out

41

If there are ghosts in Arizona, they are in Prescott.

Wonderful stories from around the state, told by credible people, describe feelings, sensations, or noises that cannot be easily explained away. One woman we respect, who lived near Marble Canyon, described watching her cat's eyes track to and fro the pacing of someone or something she herself couldn't see. A journalist told me about a Tucson house, so oppressive in a way he could not articulate, that turned out to have been the site of a murder. But the only experience

OCTOBER

I have had with someone who may not still be alive in the traditional sense was in Prescott.

The Hotel Vendome sits just off Courthouse Square, appropriately next to an old funeral home. When I worked for KTVK-TV as the northern Arizona reporter, we went to Prescott one Halloween to do a ghost story there.

Scottish tradition starts a fable by intoning "Once, about 200 years ago . . ." But this would have been more recent. At the end of the 19th century, a woman named Abbie, ill with tuberculosis, waited in Room 16 for her husband to return from getting her medicine. When he did not return, she and her cat allegedly sank into despair and decline and finally died there.

An earlier owner described to me some of the actions the staff attributed to Abbie. The call bell behind the desk would show someone in Room 16 needing service, even when the room was empty. Maids would go up to find the television blaring. Guests would wake up in the night to find the bathroom door locked from the inside and water running in the tub. All satisfactorily unnerving, but benign.

I have told my own children that, as a woman who can't explain how a document is faxed, I cannot dismiss the idea that many things I don't see or understand do exist. Radio waves. Cell phone service. Dog whistles. So far be it from me to say there is no such thing as ghosts.

Once, when my sister stayed at the Hotel Vendome with a group, several of the guests remarked on the very cold spot on the stairs. But only those few felt it. Doesn't extreme cold indicate the presence of a spirit? And did those who picked up on it have a talent just like someone with perfect pitch? Some people have better eyesight than others; maybe some have better spirit sight.

The hotel is a lovely old building, with a wide welcoming porch and cozy lobby. Upstairs, a broad hallway runs to the gallery overlooking the street. It's a building that could fit right in any quaint town back east or production of *The Music Man*.

For my television report, we did our live shot in Room 16 on Halloween night and had already decided to stay the night there. It isn't a large room; a bed takes up most of the floor space. Nothing creaked or groaned; everything seemed fresh and unblemished by dark forces. I was intrigued by the idea of a ghostly encounter. My husband and I made a few bad jokes about it and fell asleep.

Sometime in the early morning hours, I heard Tom drop his keys on the dresser and wondered why he had found it necessary to go out to the car in the dead of night. I turned my head to see he was fast asleep on the pillow next to me. Without moving, I decided Abbie must be looking for attention. I must confess when it came right down to it, I was terrified I would see her.

So I thought to her: "Abbie, if you are here, I'm a little scared. So how about if we both just recognize each other as beloved children of God and leave it at that?" Half waiting for a light to blink, or the door to slam, or worse, to feel a hand on my throat, I lay still. Nothing happened. While I waited, I wondered how much of my worldview I would have to revise if I were confronted with proof of Abbie's ability to interact with me. Would I tell people? Would they believe me? What would it do to my beliefs about heaven and angels and all, if anything? Eventually, I fell asleep.

Certainly I could have dreamed I heard those keys. That possibility is increased by the local curator and others not being able to find anything in records or the cemeteries to indicate Abbie even existed. Imagination is powerful — maybe even if I didn't think I wanted to run into Abbie, part of my subconscious liked the idea. I would not say for sure I met a ghost.

But I would not say I didn't.

A few years ago, I was visiting Charleston, South Carolina, and took a tour of the old dungeon where patriots and pirates alike had been housed. A staff member said that if you pointed your camera at one particular dark and empty area, sometimes the developed photo would show a figure. One did — a dimly outlined man in an old-fashioned shirt, gathered at the neck. I won't say for sure it's a doomed spirit.

But I won't say it isn't.

I think it's interesting that even though there is no record of Abbie, she lingers in legend. We want to believe. Maybe just as my kids now like to do what they call "creeping themselves out," there's a human fascination with things going bump in the night. Maybe it's just plain more interesting than there being only three dimensions and discernible beings.

There are researchers who make a life's study of measuring energies and frequencies, trying to ferret out life in another realm co-existing with our own. I guess I've learned I don't have the fortitude to stand a close encounter of the ghostly kind. But if you do, I'd love to hear about it.

village of the past

42

Aged markers
relate mystery
and history at
Scottsdale's
Pioneer
Cemetery.

You can visit a lot of fascinating people you'll never meet, just about a mile north of Scottsdale Fashion Square mall.

There you'll find, tucked away near 64th Street, the anomaly of Camelback Pioneer Cemetery: rustic, spare, and unpretentious land nestled in a neighborhood of very high-end homes.

For mystery and history, nothing beats a cemetery. Tubac, Williams, and Payson all have good ones to wander through, but the juxtaposition of valet-parking malls and these former area residents make this Scottsdale one particularly compelling. Cemeteries exist for those who like questions more than answers. Villages of the past, peopled with silent storytellers, cemeteries let you visit, and wonder.

A nearby resident told me the Camelback cemetery began when early homeowners needed a place to inter Mexican servants who died. Since then, it's become a highly desirable piece of real estate. A board decides who deserves to move in.

If you rate, you get a final resting place in the center of the city that feels like the middle of nowhere. With some fascinating neighbors. Like Joe "Cheyenne" Kiser, whose monument sits surrounded by a rusty iron fence with a bucking bronco welded on — kind of a New Orleans-gone-rodeo look. It celebrates his being World Champion Cowboy in 1923; the dates show he would have been 27 then. He lies buried next to a couple named Ives, who were about his age. Was he a brother to the wife?

Down a few rows is Elmer Powell, who I wish were able to tell me some of his stories; he was on the Bataan Death March as a prisoner of war. I like reading the stone's inscription, "We miss you, Dad."

And Bess Burkett told her husband (and the world) "I Love You" on his headstone; Robert was only 41 when he died. Of what, I wonder.

The saddest to me is Laura Dunn Stanley, who died at age 36, the same day as her 6-month-old son Riley. "Mother and Baby" is incised into the stone. Was it a car accident? A flu epidemic? I feel sorry for P.O. Stanley, who outlived his wife and son by almost 50 years. I wonder how often he came here.

Just as interesting, but more enigmatic, are the plots to the west of these. Probably those first servants, I'm guessing, but most are anonymous by now. Names scratched in concrete covering the graves or carved in splintery wooden crosses have worn away. This is harsher than unmarked graves; someone made the effort to pay tribute to these people, and time has taken them off the roster.

One marker's inscription in green paint has washed off; a whole row of white crosses have just blackened, dripping stains where names and dates must have been. Juan Montiel does have a hand-carved cross, showing he lived until 1969. Another cross has an arm broken off; I hope it's from weathered workmanship rather than from vandalism.

There's no parking lot, but there's no lock on the gate. Traipsing down the rows always feels a bit like trespassing; since I have no relatives or friends here, I'm an uninvited guest. At the same time, I feel anyone who comes to acknowledge and pay tribute must be welcome. Someone took the care to put up and maintain these monuments, and the least we can do is read them.

All the stories here, all the lives! The obscure maid now sharing space with prominent Herbergers and religious leaders whose monuments are as impressive as any home. Here at Camelback Pioneer Cemetery, the poor are as interesting as the rich resting next to them. No one is prettier, more clever, or more important.

Even in less historic memorials, I enjoy seeing what was vital enough to people to include in their final signoff. In a Tucson cemetery I love a Mrs. Sanders' stone saying, "I have loved the stars too deeply ever to be fearful of the night." Puts death in a nice perspective.

Visiting a cemetery also gives the best vantage point for peering beyond the veil separating us from those who have gone on ahead. I remember when my cousin Stephanie and her husband Dennis lost their baby Matthew only days after his birth. All the family members who could gathered at our grandparents' plot in the Sedona cemetery. We stood in a half-circle around the small hole in the raw red dirt while Matthew's Uncle Michael gave a eulogy.

It's impossible to be amid such palpable grief without hurting. Looking up toward the cliffs, looking at anything in an effort to keep from crying, I saw more than rock. It was as if in the bluest sky, above the red formations, were the matriarch Sedona, her husband, my father's folks, even Matthew. They looked across at our half-circle from an arc of their own, making it whole.

At Camelback Pioneer Cemetery I get a glimpse of the complete circle. I see servants as beloved as masters, unmarked crosses saying as much in a different way as the polished granite markers. People die, but can still be present, and can still teach something about equality in eternity.

I have said that I would like one of two epitaphs to commemorate my time here: either "Dressed to minimize figure flaws," or "Celebrate . . . Remember . . . Believe." But if I don't get to micromanage my memorial, it's interesting to know that I might inspire a different type of story, a thought-starter, in anonymity.

Unlike old New Orleans, where one gets to occupy the burial vault for a year and a day, people who were interred here remain. And while the "dust to dust" part of the journey is clear, it's equally true that everyone who is still part of this visible place, who shares either biographical information or enigmatic silence, is not truly forgotten.

in brighty's steps

43

If you have visited the North Rim of the Grand Canyon, nine other Canyon visitors have not. Which makes you a member of a substantially smaller group of Arizona residents, or United States citizens, to have gotten lost in the view from the higher side.

Brighty's statue resides at the North Rim Lodge, from which visitors can gaze into the Grand Canyon.

The North Rim's 8,000-foot elevation gives you an extra thousand over the South Rim — hard on hikers, a blessing for photographers. I'm astonished to be able to see all the way to Flagstaff's San Francisco Peaks when I look south over the Canyon.

My father and I have brought my children here for their first visit — actually Sedona was here when she was just a few months old, but of course she remembers nothing. We bring along now the book *Brighty of the Grand Canyon* that my father had bought and signed for her then. Taking turns, we read as we ride, so that they will know they are walking where the friendly, determined little burro stepped and grazed almost a century ago.

Because of snow, the North Rim is closed to all but a small staff from mid-October to mid-May. It's last call now, and the breezes that come to meet us as we walk to our cabin give a hint of what this same wind will feel like whisking snow in another month. Having our own front porch with sturdy rocking chairs charms us, and we all watch with equally young eyes the deer that comes to nibble on the grass out in front.

We can't meet the real Brighty on the Kaibab Trail, so we make introductions in the North Rim Lodge lobby to the little burro's bronze statue in the window room. While people move steadily to the windows bigger than my house to observe the scenic drama outside, we detour to the corner where Brighty stands recreated, bristly and exuding cheerful energy. The bronze statue's patina is dark, except for his nose, which has been lovingly polished golden by generations of children.

We talk about, but do not see, Kaibab squirrels, which have evolved to a different animal than their cousins just across the Canyon's chasm, their high white tails making for better camouflage in the snowdrifts. We muse about Teddy Roosevelt hunting here with Brighty and how the president created the national park where we walk. My father points out fir trees and the difference between them and ponderosa pines.

That's when I remember him taking a few pine needles from a branch on another northern Arizona trip and putting the ends in his mouth.

"Always tastes like Christmas," he had said.

And I stared as if he'd plucked a cigarette wrapper from a gutter — you don't eat things that are just hanging around outside! But I'm a city girl, to whom Outside means Dirty. To my father, with the winds of northern Arizona still blowing through his soul from childhood, Outside is Clean.

That night at dinner, we notice that ours are the only children in the room. We realize also that this is an area that many families probably can't visit. You would need a dependable vehicle, enough vacation time, and the cash to cover meals away. A lot of Arizona youth is not in that position and will not stand at these same incredible windows, or hike down the trail, absorbing this very significant part of their state.

And that's too bad. Everyone needs a way to test his or her own mettle as they grow, to dare themselves, bounce their spirits off different surfaces to see how the sounds change. Back when they could run off to sea or go west, they could get outside the system without going against it. Now there are no openings for cabin boys posted on the Department of Economic Security jobs board.

I'm not saying Wasn't It Perfect Then and Ain't It Awful Now. In the 1940s, one of my father's boyhood friends was victim of what was called the Dollar Bill Murder in the sweet spot of Mountain View, California. But because parents more than children see monsters in the bushes now, many children get the message that it's safer to be racing the courses of video games than out on a real bicycle.

And without being outside, so much is lost. The innate awareness of lengthening days and outdoor scents that change with seasons. The knowledge of physical limits — I didn't get that until I rafted the Canyon in my 20s. In these times, wading in creeks and picking wild berries is as much a part of most childhoods as gathering eggs or driving the tractor from Grandpa's lap. Unless it's virtual reality, it probably won't happen.

Surely only a few details of this North Rim visit will remain as active memories for my children, they're still so young. It's impossible to know if they will include soaking in the stars with their Poppa, taking the same trail Brighty trod, or just leaving the CD case in the hotel room and eating fries with ketchup. But certainly I hope this time be stored away to have some impact on their souls, another puzzle piece that will add shape to their concept of their own place in the larger natural world, and what a vast and wondrous world it is.

Until I have a fund to help bring all children to actual wilderness, I have to remember that even cities house rich deposits of nature. There are clouds that make shapes, sunshine going south for the winter and lighting different walls, the scent of pending rain, and rocks with different colors and origins. Anything may help instill an awareness of organic creations, untouched by man; may help create in children a curiosity that will someday lead them on their own to places like the North Rim, where they will test their muscles and wits and know the frisky lure of taking the trail, walking in spirit with Brighty.

honoring the veterans

44

"Veteran" brings a different image to each of us.

For my parents, it's the proud men, marching in long-ago parades, who fought in World War I and those a few years older than themselves who came back from World War II. In the background, they hear the strains of "Roses of Picardy" and "The White Cliffs of Dover."

Some think of Navajo Code Talkers in World War II; some now think of yellow ribbons waving on fences for Gulf War soldiers.

I think of Jim Randall. And the sound track I hear is by Santana.

Neither flags nor honors, like the Vietnam Memorial in Phoenix, left, can ease all the bitter memories.

Randall was a news photographer who worked with me in Tucson television; we covered a Veterans Day parade together not long after he came to KGUN. I remember him, kneeling in front of a tank rolling down the parade route, and later thinking it was a metaphor for how his Vietnam combat tour still bore down on him, threatening to crush him under the weight of memory. He introduced me to Irish Mist, a mead-based liqueur that was his drink of choice in post-war gatherings called "firebases," where veterans would meet to share and purge their memories.

I went the day before Veterans Day to the Vietnam Veterans Memorial by the Arizona Capitol, as a tribute.

Randall missed the televised walk on the moon because he was patrolling the perimeter, far from electricity. He missed the birth of his first son, and less than 24 hours from the jungle to a Detroit hospital, he was told his son was damaged and his wife might die because of a doctor's inattention. He said later he couldn't understand not being allowed to kill this man, who had almost ruined his family, when he was encouraged to kill strangers every day.

He came home with all the ingredients for a time bomb inside him, and sometimes those volatile elements almost detonated. He played a lot of guitar, and the music worked with his wife's love to heal him.

So when he played at Nam Jam in Tucson, lots of us went to Reid Park hear him play with his band.

Vietnam veterans come in all shapes and types, but the ones drawn to Nam Jam tended to wear black, tattoos and carry a little extra weight. And, in some cases, a big chip on their shoulders. To a civilian, it looked like blame that they were the only combatants who weren't welcomed when they came back.

These men have always prompted both guilt and fascination in me. They have gone to the absolute edge of life and sanity, and, having peered over the precipice and survived to tell about it, they possess something few of my generation ever will. Their tours prove what they're made of.

Given the choice, they all say that combat's a privilege they never wanted; they'd rather use bungee jumping or running marathons to show they're tough enough than to have had their cards validated in such a harsh way. But the survivors do celebrate their shared passage now in a way they didn't used to.

Bill Pritzen, a friend of Randall's, said that sometime since the Persian Gulf War of 1991, Vietnam has become acceptable, even vogue, in some circles. After being spit on and cursed at upon returning, Vietnam vets are getting admiration and curiosity. Vietnam wannabes began to emerge, until the Vietnam Veterans' Association actually had to start asking for discharge papers with membership applications. Pritzen credits the VVA with helping him and lots of other veterans come to terms with their tours of duty.

But like an apology 20 years after an infidelity in a marriage, this attitude change doesn't erase the hurt and alienation. And the lack of welcome was only half the problem. Time heals some wounds; others slowly infect and kill. Pritzen said some who came back from Vietnam still haven't left it.

"You can go to the other end of the display tent and watch guys on their knees bawling; some never let it go. I don't think they know it's possible."

The display tent at Nam Jam, set up beyond the bandshell, exhibited a visual summary of their combat tours via relics contributed by veterans. Randall had donated a few things, and he walked slowly through the very temporary museum.

Outside stood a helicopter, the same kind that carried most of them incountry. While Randall made peace with his time there, he still has issues here:

"You don't forget what it felt like. I forgave the enemy when I went back there a couple of years ago; they didn't want us there in the first place. I don't forgive the government."

Just inside the tent we saw a display of machine guns. Randall pointed out the M-60 with its bristling loops of ammunition. "That's what I used to hump through the jungle."

"What does it weigh?"

He considered.

"Depends on how long you humped it."

He looked at poems, snapshots of impossibly young-looking GIs carrying out forgotten routines in barren camps. The stove that burned a clear invisible flame stirred stories in him. So did what looked like playing cards with skulls and regiments printed on them.

"Death cards," Randall said. "When a unit would go through and kick somebody's ass real bad, a lot of times they'd flip these around and let 'em know who did it."

A brass bracelet made by a member of the Montagnard tribe in the highlands of Vietnam brings back bad memories.

"They were allies. I had one of those bracelets. But when it came time to get out, the government had time to get out the bigwigs and their gold, but left the 'Nards on their own. That's the kind of thing I can't forgive."

The shrine with burning candles, a first letter home from a young soldier, show how distant a place these men returned from. Somehow Randall's recovered, not just from the red talons of memory that used to score his sleep, but from the chemicals that caused the rashes, aches, and burning.

Bitterness seeps from many sources: race, military service, divorce. Most people move on and are stronger in Hemingway's broken places. But there was talk at Nam Jam about a fellow veteran who overdosed in a Las Vegas hotel room just the month before, still fighting a war he couldn't get out of.

It's odd to realize that the Vietnam conflict is chronologically further removed from my children than World War II was from me. And for many, even among the veterans, it is past tense. Not everyone still has unspeakable memories he can't shake or addictions needed to hold back the nightmares. But in their solidarity, surrounded by gritty dust and Santana music, some held themselves apart from civilians. "We are not like you," their silence said. "We are not fortunate sons. You can't understand that. You didn't used to try, and we won't help you now."

No one can make it better by holding hands and singing "Kum Ba Yah." Or say, "I know how you feel," to these men, and be right. Only "never again" about turning our backs on troops who went to serve.

We can thank those veterans we meet. We can toast their courage with Irish Mist. We can pray that those who haven't sought the rough healing presence of fellow veterans will, at some point. Because you could tell by some of the granite expressions on the faces around the tent that the rage and confusion and grief of war don't fade with time. War is like Randall's M-60. It gets heavier the longer you carry it.

eyes full of sonnets

45

Someone's grandma should have said it, and maybe did: "If you can't be happy, make someone else happy." On holidays when I've been away from family or lacking a significant other, I could get pretty morose. So I would buy small boxes of chocolates and go to a nursing home to be of some use to someone.

People who looked as if they hadn't known a vigorous day in their lives stared at, past, or through me, slumped sentries in the hall. I walked through this gauntlet, smiling. What now? Walk up to a nurse and say, "Hi, I'm a do-gooder and want to cheer someone up without being patronizing?" I found an aide; I asked who didn't get visitors. Why did I talk then around a lump in my throat?

That has happened every time I've made this kind of visit: to Mr. Powell, whose wife had died after 60 years together; to Alice, who was sure her daughter was coming to visit because she lived right here in town (the nurse said the daughter never came). I've met Caroline, who assured me her father had a big ranch in Prescott and was coming to fetch her in the sleigh. I remember Millie, who was so lively describing early Phoenix and walking home after a young man got fresh with her in his Model A that I could almost see the girl she had been. I've talked

The man's hands gently framed a visitor's face as he must have a daughter or granddaughter.

213

with, or to, quiet women who watched me from eyes so full of expression that it's amazing their mouths didn't release it in sonnets.

Then there's my ghost of Christmas Future. She was a woman in the center of a rec room, bouncing up and down in her wheelchair. When she saw me come in, she pointed sharply, ordering me to fetch that pillow, bring that card from the top of the television. Then she wanted the VCR and the cable box. I realized this wasn't going to work and explained other people needed those things left alone.

"But we need this cleaned up!" she snapped, her arms shaking in frustration. I looked at her. I saw someone trying to control something, accomplish something. But she couldn't. She'd been brought down from the heyday of managing a home full of people and could only try to recreate the old productivity by proxy.

I knelt down next to her.

"I bet you've always been a very busy person, haven't you?" I asked. She stopped bouncing and looked at me sternly.

"Well, there's always a tremendous amount to get done."

Sometimes when I'm on full-throttle, self-absorbed with list-making and errand-running, high on accomplishing, I remember her. If I put more stock in getting a lot done than in learning to appreciate whatever a moment offers, I'm heading for that center stage in a rec room.

Then there was the man who looked like Rip Van Winkle, hunched in a vinyl chair by the dining room. His mouth puckered shut as if pulled by a drawstring, but maybe it was to prevent his full white beard from drifting in, like clouds into a cave.

I always fumble my opening line as awkwardly as walking up to someone at a junior high dance. I asked him what he had done before he retired, and somewhere in his mumbled syllables I made out "fireman."

What should I do then? Pretend to understand? Tell jokes? I explained that my grandpa used to live in a home like this, and I couldn't always get in to visit him. This year, I didn't have any grandpa to visit, and I figured someone would let me come by and talk for a bit.

He looked at me, and I gave him the little box of Russell Stover chocolates and said I bet all the nurses admired that beard. I couldn't tell if he heard me or not.

I said a few more things, picked up my purse, and got ready to stand. He reached out, then, and gently touched my chin with a framing hand. It was a gesture I'm sure a daughter or granddaughter felt dozens of times, and it came with the kindest, clearest gaze I've ever seen. He offered the kind of comforting touch that is at the heart of every grandparent legend. For a minute, I was a granddaughter again.

I always leave feeling tremulous, like I've been through something but can't tell what. It's not a reaction to the people just waiting for something — or worse, waiting for nothing. It's not about my own fear that someday I'll be without control, or hope. I sense in my reaction more a bone-deep awe, an honored and aware feeling of being in the presence of something sacred.

I think interacting with someone in its purest form, without motive or history creating static, touches the soul. Going to someone to let them know they matter purely because they exist, not because they write your paycheck or will compliment you in turn, always reaches my core. I realize, like Emily in *Our Town* did after she died, how incredibly precious our small moments are.

There are years when Thanksgiving passes and I don't go to a nursing home. I am poorer when that happens, because I miss that pure and perfect meeting with someone I don't know.

indian thanksgiving

46 When we fourth-graders were taught "Brave and High-Souled Pilgrims," I don't remember us noticing that Indians were not mentioned, any more than I wondered what being "high-souled" actually entailed.

It wasn't until years later, driving from Tuba City in Navajoland the day before the holiday that I wondered how today's tribes feel about the holiday.

Certainly a revisionist history would probably present the story differently from what we were taught: hardy Pilgrims prayed and worked to not only stay alive but prevail over a harsh land and thanked God by hosting a banquet for native tribes. The poor newcomers pretty much stumbled about, invitations to starvation, sustained by the Indians' patient education about corn and squash. So is Thanksgiving in Arizona like Jefferson Davis's birthday to descendents of slaves — something that exists, but hardly warrants gladness? A bitter irony, celebrating the beginning of the end for the tribes who sustained the newcomers?

Depends on whom you ask.

One Hopi woman I spoke with, Susie Kuyvaya, said that while the Indian contributions have been pretty widely ignored, "There was nothing to be done about it. Hopis were never outspoken. The main view

A child plays at Young's Farm in a pumpkin field.

among the older people is that none of this [Thanksgiving] exists. At my grandmother's, it's just another day. A pot of beans and fry bread."

She said, because of school holidays, Thanksgiving has crept into the lives of younger families — including hers.

"We're kind of progressive. We want to do something. We have turkey, pumpkin pie. Cranberries are hard to find here."

(Which is actually in keeping with history; I found out from visiting the Ocean Spray site near Plymouth that pilgrims avoided cranberries, what they called "bogberries," because the sugar needed to make them tasty was more expensive than the dish was worth.)

Another grandmother, Harriet Manuel, does celebrate Thanksgiving, gathering as much of her Pima family as she can in her Gila reservation home. With five grown children, this can be quite a group.

"I know there are families who don't want to be part of it," she says, "but we always have. Turkey with dressing, mashed potatoes and yams, pie with whipped cream." The only difference between her table and a Norman Rockwell painting is the tortillas instead of rolls.

To some, the name of the holiday is not as important as the meaning behind it.

"If you ask Hopis who don't celebrate Thanksgiving if they celebrate harvest, the answer is yes," Harriet says. "The good crop; food to gather, grow and preserve. We give thanks, also, for family gathered together."

She describes the celebration that predated the Plymouth Rock gathering by centuries. Depending on the region, corn, squash, or rice was part of the harvest celebration dinner. "Iroquois had maple, strawberries, and green corn."

Patti Talahongva said it was hard as a child in school to hear the story of the first Thanksgiving focused on the Pilgrims.

"It was as if the Pilgrims said, 'Oh, better invite a few Indians, too,'" she says. "My understanding is that tribes would have had to show the settlers how to grow new types of food. Corn is a whole phenomenon. You don't just throw seeds; you plant them in shallow soil. It doesn't just grow like wild rice or berries. You need to be there; need to pray over it and tend it."

She hopes the contributions to the first white Americans become increasingly recognized. Other ethnic groups have holidays honoring their leaders, but on Thanksgiving, Indians seem token. But if she's disappointed about the short shrift Indians receive on the only holiday which even mentions them, Talahongva still celebrates Thanksgiving.

"Sometimes it's important to give up the differences," she says. "We can all give thanks for being together."

In this land of the melting pot, Thanksgiving is an accommodating holiday, like the elastic waists that make room for our deliberate excess. My friend Bessie Cano is from the Philippines; her traditional Thanksgiving includes lechon and pansit: roast pig and a noodle dish brought from her homeland. My friend Daryn Kagan, who loves to tell about sending a boyfriend to the emergency room after cooking him a turkey dinner, says Thanksgiving is still her favorite holiday "because it's all about being together with family and friends, with none of the commercialism that threatens to engulf Christmas."

Odd, but our celebrated traditions of Thanksgiving Day were once alien and new to the Pilgrims. Turkeys were new and wild birds from the thick forests of this strange land, while squash and corn added new ingredients to recipes carefully copied back in England.

If there is a traditional theme of Thanksgiving, maybe it is the adaptability to celebrate with whatever is at hand. If your family is far away, you join friends at their table. If you are used to cranberries, never mind that they weren't on the original menu. For the Pilgrims, new foods and new friends combined for the age-old appreciation of harvest and being alive to see it.

As some have learned all they needed to know in kindergarten, much of what I believe worthy of saying has been penned by singer/songwriter Don Henley.

In his song "My Thanksgiving," Henley writes:

I've got great expectations,
I've got family and friends,
I've got satisfying work,
And a back that bends.
For every breath,
For every day of living,
This is my Thanksgiving.

Beyond the friends, food, and family, the rest is mere detail. But when we roll the credits, I hope we include the native tribes who helped keep the newcomers alive to create the tradition. Their hospitality is the original sweetness in Thanksgiving; the Reddi-Wip came later.

civility on a saucer

47 Since the first females stepped down from wagon beds and into shanties in the Arizona Territory, tea has been a ritual that has changed far less, since then, than modes of dress or transportation.

If one of those early settlers were to sit down to afternoon tea today in Tucson, Phoenix, or Flagstaff, she would be instantly comfortable: thin china cups, savories and sweets, and the light conversation of women would be the same as it was in her time.

Looking through cookbooks and collections of journals, you find

The Phoenician maintains a teatime tradition.

photographs of yesteryear's women, seeking the reassuring ritual of gathering over a cup of tea. For them, even more than for us, it was a symbol of leisure. For that single hour, they would not be up to their elbows in scalding lye or sweating over a hoe. They could, briefly, forget their lives were hard. For the time that they presided over the teapot, they were involved in the same actions as the aristocracy of England or the society ladies of Boston. Taking tea was elegant, removed from routine, and genteel. And still is today.

An aficionado of afternoon tea can travel the state and experience different details of the beloved event: some small teahouses like Tea and Sympathy in Flagstaff, or Teeter House in downtown Phoenix, offer delightful menus with unexpected selections like chilled peach soup in summer and hearty meat pastries in winter. As some have said about other more earthy pursuits, the worst tea I ever had was terrific. But the best is at the Phoenician Hotel in Scottsdale.

Not just the best in Arizona. Better than at the Ritz Hotel in Boston, Windsor Court in New Orleans, the Four Seasons in Southern California, even the venerable Plaza Hotel in New York. When my sister and I have sampled afternoon tea in other cities, it invariably falls short of the Phoenician.

It's all about detail. The Phoenician doesn't miss on a single point, while everyone else drops the tea ball somewhere. It might be either sugar cubes, or even packets, instead of glistening crystals scooped with a tiny spoon. Some places don't bother with a sterling lemon squeezer. Not everyone offers six varieties of sandwiches — with seconds. Pastries sometimes are served, fait accompli, three on a plate, instead of the Ziegfeld finale on a silver tray that comes at the Phoenician: cream-filled swans, chocolate-dipped strawberries, fruit tarts, mocha layers, pistachio bites, and others so delectable that only dignity prevents selecting one of everything.

Music is not necessary for a fine tea, but it's nice. Live music is perfect. At the Phoenician, the harpist or chamber quartet or pianist is accompanied by the soft whisper of the nearby fountain. A dulcet civility instantly overlays even the most mundane conversations.

I once heard of a woman who has a standing reservation at the Phoenician for afternoon tea every week. I want to be her in my next life. There is something beguiling about the ritual of the silver strainer laid over the cup to catch leaves as tea is poured; the delicacy of small sandwiches, garnished with bits of bright herbs; the deliberate excess of clotted cream, buttery and thick on a split scone. One is charmed and soothed at the same time.

Because tea makes people feel so indulged, the interaction is also elevated to a finer level. Confidences are shared more quickly. We become our best selves. We have time to talk about philosophy and ideals. We feel pampered and maybe figure we must be worthwhile, or we wouldn't be sitting deep in a brocade chair while people bring us more sweets.

For several years, the book group to which I belong has made a holiday pilgrimage to the Phoenician for afternoon tea. We bring tiny gifts and dress in reds and golds. The tradition introduces the Christmas season and has come to represent a lovely rest in the seasonal music of our lives, before it accelerates to a frantic crescendo of preparation and festivity. We share poems, thoughts, or ideas for gifts, and we laugh.

And just as our foremothers received its reprieve from churning or soap-making, tea grants a respite for us. When we are selecting our Earl Gray or the lemon curd for our scones, we are not jockeying for mini-van parking at a soccer match, or arguing with an indifferent clerk at a bank over service charges. We are women of leisure and refinement. We have made time to dress in our best and sally forth with no greater goal than conviviality and light nourishment. And not only from the food.

Last year as I was walking in and saw the women gathered, I flashed forward to a future for which I hope: decades of this same group meeting here for holiday tea. Someday, if we're fortunate enough to live so long, one or more of us may rely on a cane as we walk in. I wonder which of us will be the first to lose a husband. I wonder what tales we will exchange, of children then grown, perhaps traveling overseas. We might share photographs of a first grandchild. And while we age to the outside world, we will each see in turn Jennifer, Cathy, Susan, or Janean, just as we look to one another today.

That timelessness is much of the appeal of afternoon tea. The water table may fall, different world leaders may horrify us. Skin will not always be as smooth and hair will not always be as shiny and thick as they are today. But there will always be afternoon tea, with many of the same trappings as Queen Victoria enjoyed, unaltered by microwaves, technology, or time. It is a reminder that all is not lost; that some things do remain the same in the ways that are most important.

When I look up from a plate of miniature sandwiches at the faces of the women with whom I am growing older, I still feel like a little girl at a tea party. Worries are suspended; we are cosseted, away from all things plebian. Afternoon tea gives us a brief shimmering golden time to see and feel only what is good and beautiful, fortifying ourselves to go out once again and deal with the rest.

smile, darn it

48

It begins innocently enough. Proud parents want family and friends far and near to see the cutest baby in the world. A photo goes out in the annual holiday card.

As the children, and the years, multiply, things get a little more complicated. First, they're afraid of the camera. Then boys go through a stage where they show all their teeth when asked to smile. If they do get past that grimace, it's in time to try to cover blemishes, to hide braces behind grimly closed smiles, and then simply to want to be somewhere else the

The Schnebly family holiday card, 1965.

DECEMBER

day the Christmas card picture is taken. Growing up in a family with egos the size of emu eggs, it wasn't enough to be clean and smiling. We did theme photos.

Over the years, we dabbed our noses in flour and posed with cookie cutters, gathered around the holiday dinner table, borrowed vaudeville hats and wore red, white and blue. Evidence proves that once, during the Partridge Family era, we even set up as a family band in the living room. I'm the one in a polyester vest with a tambourine. We did Western, which meant Lyle wore his Frye boots and the rest of us made do with jeans.

No photographer took more than one turn behind our camera. The only constant was that we smiled. Through clenched teeth, hissing, "Is someone blocking the light on my face?" "Lyle, are you making bunny ears?" At some point my mother would become convinced she didn't show, and at intervals her plaintive, "Can you see me?" would float over the back row.

My dad tried to joke the troops into a jovial mood. The troops generally acted rude, fighting for face time and rejecting suggestions of group-mindedness. The tension thickened like the seasonal inversion layer of smog over Phoenix.

And that was only the beginning. When proofs came back, the gloves came off. Eyeing one another like feral dogs over the kill, we gathered with marking pens to vote. "What do you mean, that's a finalist? I look completely startled!" "We can't use this; my shoulders look narrow." "Who voted for this where I have lizard lips?" We assigned point values, we did runners-up. Finally, the parent most fed up with the shenanigans announced a winner, which was sent off to be printed into 200 images of a family happy to be together.

What a hassle, what a pain, we all said. And yet when we brought friends home for the first time, we invariably ended up in the hall, where each decade of cards occupies its own frame.

See . . . here's how I looked in braces. That's the year we got our dog.

Look at the big hair! There's Mom wearing her Jackie Kennedy hat.

The frames hold a family's history under glass, and it isn't over yet. The first grandchild appeared. More figures are added, with all of us dressed for a wedding. This is real life, so several former spouses have vanished, and another wedding shows up in a few years. A dozen (or so) of us now gather and grin annually.

We are products of our upbringing. Now I am the one, starting around May, who mentally scans the plans of the next months to see where our own family's photo op might arise. I knew my maternal chromosomes were rightly aligned the first time I picked a picture that wasn't the best of me, because it was better of toddler Sedona.

Being the Arizona enthusiast I am, I've dreamed of going on location, but that has turned out to be less than practical. The only time we tend to all be together feeling photogenic is at my brother's house in Long Beach. So we have two photos taken in Oak Creek Canyon, and the rest at home or in California.

But when it comes down to it, the background isn't as important as I once thought it would be. The pictures show when someone gets glasses, gets gray, gets pregnant. A setting is, as my sister Laurie says, so much velvet. This year we managed to gather in New River, and with cousin Mary Ann taking the picture, we all tried to smile while watching her 2-year-old son stay an appropriate distance from a large furry tarantula.

With children has come insight. I understand why my mother never suggested doing a nativity scene with the newest baby in a manger. And why she didn't like the idea of all of us facing away from the camera. I see why she put up with the peace signs, foot-dragging, and sibling-pinching at DeGrazia's studio and at the Arizona Inn. At Christmas you give your greatest gift: your family.

And now we Heidingers, too, have filled the first decade frame hung in our hallway, tracing the unfurling of another generation. Someday our son, Rye, will show a girlfriend how his hair stood straight up when he was a baby; our daughter, Sedona will point out the beloved family

227

poodle, Happy Jack. The cycle continues.

Sit up and smile, darn it.

I'm good in that one.

Merry Christmas, from our house to yours.

Boats bear lights and decorations for Lake Havasu City's holiday parade.

chirstmas, quietly

49

It's beginning to look a lot like Christmas . . . but you can tell only if you've lived here awhile.

Growing up in Arizona with picture books of carolers swathed in scarves, bright new sleds under the tree, and lights reflecting off white front yards, I always felt a bit left out playing outside on Christmas without being told to wear a sweater.

We don't have traditional wassailing weather, although my mother always reminded us that our climate was actually closer to Bethlehem's

229

and therefore in keeping with the true holiday. While the secular holiday traditions aren't the easy clichés they are back East, they seep as deeply into your consciousness as any Currier and Ives print once you live them.

Luminarias, for one — golden glowing beacons that represent the path to heaven. And how egalitarian, these simple sturdy brown paper bags weighted with sand and lit with votive candles. So cheap it's almost free, as if illustrating you can't buy your way to paradise.

Traditions for lots of Arizonans include making tamales. I marvel at families willing to come together and work all day like that. My mother always baked the braided Czechoslovakian bread, hoska — frosted and full of raisins — for Christmas breakfast, which my sister has taken on. The rest of us just have to show up to sing "Happy Birthday" to Jesus.

Stitched onto my image of Christmas is the Man in the Maze, the Tohono O'odham symbol of a stick figure standing on the edge of a labyrinth. I went to San Xavier Mission one bitterly windy grey afernoon to find out about the Feast of San Xavier, which is celebrated this time of year. Gene Enis, a large man with strength in his mild voice and eyes, took us up on a hill overlooking the festival and explained a tradition centuries old: how wood for the festival cooking fire is always gathered from a certain grove; a committee of 12 couples organizes the prayer services and dances; grandmothers and new babies alike arrive early and stay late.

At the base of the hill under a time-battered ramada, a band scratched out whimsically catchy music. Children in bright sweaters danced together in the dirt while their parents circled on the cement. Gene Enis talked slowly and softly. He was giving a gift telling these stories. I got a sense of San Xavier as far more than the "White Dove of the Desert" pictured on scenic calendars; it gives a vital center for the tribe's culture and customs. I hope Gene Enis someday gets to pass on the red ribbon of a San Xavier committee member to a young son as his father did to him and tell the story of the man in the maze seeking the center all his life.

On Arizona's western border, Lake Havasu City gives you two for one in its parade of lights: the decorated boats themselves, and their reflections in the water of the Colorado River under London Bridge.

Up north in Flagstaff, the holiday season begins with the lighting of the huge tree on the Northern Arizona University campus. (A nice sense of place: It shares a lawn with R.C. Gorman's wonderful sculpture of his father, a Navajo Code Talker.) And for a sprig of traditional holiday feeling, at the Grand Canyon Deer Farm between Flagstaff and Williams, real deer curl gracefully into the snow, waiting for visitors with cups of nuggets to feed them. (The farm's owners scatter shelters about, and I always want to herd the deer toward them, or onto straw, yet they persist in living as they have for centuries in the wild, settling wherever they happen to be.)

Hayrides through the Winterhaven neighborhood are part of a Tucson Christmas. As a teenager, my best friend lived in that neighborhood, which mandates decorating your home for the holidays. We gathered at her home to paint paper plates like penny candy for the rim of the King's life-sized gingerbread house. My brother almost proposed to his wife in Winterhaven, but changed his mind "because once we'd done that, it would be odd to go back to 'check out that Snoopy display!'"

Red Rock Fantasy is the festival of lights at the Los Abrigados Resort in Sedona. Chillier to walk through, it's also more compact than Winterhaven. The hot drinks and individual displays competing for prizes are gorgeous in their abundance, and while purists would argue that the real red rocks cannot be improved upon, sometimes I think a lily is even more fun occasionally gilded.

To me, the hushed and humming moment before the Prescott Courthouse comes alive with light is the most thrilling holiday herald. The Courthouse Square throngs with people clutching styrofoam cups of cocoa and visiting while they wait for the chorus to start the holiday carols. Then the square sits briefly in darkness until lights ignite everywhere, winding up the granite columns, edging the gazebo, decorating the walls.

It's like Disneyland, or an experience created to give you a sense of living in a gentler time, especially in the tree-filled lobby of the Hassayampa Hotel, which boasts the most elegantly faded gentility I know.

Many southern Arizonans count their visit to the Arizona Inn as a holiday kickoff, admiring the grand tree in the corner of the library, maybe with a quiet hour for tea in the glow of the lights.

Of course the kernel, the germ of the holiday, exists without geography. The signposts by which we know the holiday are as individual as our fingerprints. For my father, it's eggnog by the tree after Midnight Mass. For me it's writing on the box of decorations that has my father's printing in faint red ink, beginning in 1953 with brief paragraphs about our year.

And more than giving to those dear to me, it's about giving to those not dear to me. The first time my children saw the Salvation Army's red kettle, heard the ringing of their bell, and turned to me for money to push into the kettle, I couldn't speak for a minute. That had become part of holiday to them.

Arizona's traditions, from handmade luminarias to tree-lighting festivals, do have one thing in common: including, not isolating people. For all our separate ways of celebrating, we have that most important thread unifying us. We realize the color in the tapestry comes from one another, and this time of year we are better at weaving together than usual. The pattern of holidays in Arizona is not classical, nor staid: we are more what someone called "the happy band of stragglers," on our way to the year's ultimate celebration.

riding the polar express

50

As snowflakes danced down gently, we walked out onto the railway platform to see the decorated Polar Express.

The old locomotive was as festive as its namesake. In the Christmas storybook, *The Polar Express*, a young boy wakes to the whistle of a train unexpectedly waiting outside his door Christmas Eve to take him to the North Pole. He receives the First Gift of Christmas from Santa — a bell off the sleigh, with a clear sweet music only believers can hear.

From just after Thanksgiving until Christmas, the Grand Canyon

From the parlor car on the Grand Canyon Railway, Polar Express travelers see the rail yard at Williams.

DECEMBER

233

Railway in Williams does some moonlighting. You can still make the regular daily run to the Canyon's South Rim, or you can take one of two nightly trips on the Polar Express. A trip of about 30 minutes through the snowy darkness leads to a specially created North Pole stop, complete with the cookies and cocoa the children in the book enjoy during their ride.

Pulling up to the depot in light snowfall was the perfect way to step into the scene. Garlands decorate both inside and out. The lobby, with its traditional ticket booths, also sells souvenirs, and I paid just a few dollars for a huge sleigh bell like the one in the book, which jingled softly from my purse the rest of the day before coming home to add another story to our tree decorations.

Parents have raved about being able to sit in the lobby of the lovely Fray Marcos Hotel by the Grand Canyon Railway depot, enjoying their coffee, toasty warm, while watching their children gleefully play in the snowy courtyard, safely contained. The train we saw, festooned with all manner of holiday trim, is a set piece rather than transportation, but it was doing brisk business as a backdrop for photos before the morning train loaded up with passengers.

And "loaded up" is a bit misleading. During the week before Christmas, the South Rim run is sparsely settled, which is the best way to take a train ride. The conductor had time to stroll and visit, in his traditional uniform. The musician on board played requests and chatted with the children. Everyone felt special.

I find it fitting that this particular railway stands in for the storied Polar Express, because if there were ever a Mr. and Mrs. Santa, they would be the railway's founders, Max and Thelma Beigert. When you arrive in Williams and see Max and Thelma's Restaurant, it soothes with a down-home country feeling. Max and Thelma, who launched the Grand Canyon Railway in 1989, are the most gracious couple I know.

Max is a true gentleman, courtly and spare with the white-haired dignity of a lord of the manor, while Thelma is a tiny sprite who radiates maternal interest and good manners. She also gives the impression that she could engineer the most difficult project and draw the best efforts out of all involved without ever raising her voice. And the Grand Canyon Railway did not come easily into being.

Before it opened, I remember visiting the partially completed depot to do a television story. Al Richmond, who remains the official Grand Canyon Railway historian, was delighting in the newly installed bell, which issued a ring as mellow as fine brandy as it swung gently back and forth on the engine. Al was, and remains, as excited as a boy about trains.

On the inaugural run, which was a photo finish that had employees frantically wrapping up loose ends almost until it pulled from the station, fuel problems made the smoke pour out black, and the run took almost twice as long as expected. But the glitches were solved, and now the train runs as punctually as if it were somehow powered by a satellite running world time.

Trains hold a special power that makes them so much more than the sum of their parts. They bring out the eager dreamer in us, with their implied images of adventure and faraway places. The very cadence of a train, the click and sway, is both relaxing and invigorating. And the sounds! Wheels ticking the track away, the blast of whistle, the chuff of the engine . . . those are ingredients of reverie.

Once aboard, you settle into the old seats feeling like you could be your own grandparent's friend. The polished wood doors between cars say "Pullman" in bronze script. The club car, with its libations and refreshments, makes you want to rest your boot on a rail and say "gad!" about something. And the observation car, with the level of seats looking out over the top of the train, may be the best of all. From anywhere, the sensation of slowly becoming aware of motion underneath, gradually quickening, is a universal pleasure.

The tracks parallel the highway from Williams to the Canyon for the most part. Proceeding at a slower pace than by car, you can see the ponderosa pines start to enter the juniper landscape. Even with a fairly faint covering of snow, the ride is like being magically transported into a favorite childhood book.

You can, of course, ride daylight to the Canyon, disembarking with the aid of the same courteous conductor at the lovely old depot. (The only twinge is having to come in backwards for ease of pulling out again later — it feels odd.) Climbing the stone steps to one of the restaurants, taking time to gaze, photograph, and shop, you have more than three hours before leaving.

Or take the ride through the dark, shorter on scenery but longer on excitement, for the not knowing of what is outside the window you can breath on and frost.

Either way, the ride crowns the holiday season. And how fitting that Max and Thelma Beigert, who persisted in making their dream real, get to offer the Polar Express to generations of riders. I suspect that, after the ride, more people can hear the sleigh bell ring.

el tovar's holiday solitude

51

Winter in a national park eclipses the summer park experience completely. Like a chocolate bar, a breathtaking landscape shared with thousands of others means less for you. So the best place to visit, the week before Christmas, is the El Tovar hotel at the South Rim of the Grand Canyon.

I had originally intended to herald El Tovar as the perfect place to spend Christmas Day itself, but now I know that the better plan is to go when not everyone else has had the same idea. A few dozen people will dine at nearby tables, instead of a few hundred. You may actually take

The mounted heads of moose and deer wear holiday garb at El Tovar.

DECEMBER

photographs without a single person in them. The Rim Walk is deserted. And if you're lucky, the snow is falling.

It was the hushed expectant spirit that I knew would be enhanced here. The Canyon is — well, the Canyon. And El Tovar is where the finest efforts of humankind meet one of nature's master works. To stand on the third-floor balcony, framed by lightning rods, and watch the shadows and mist play below the Rim is to know the best of both.

Coming up on its first century, El Tovar, named as a salute to a Spanish explorer, exhibits the grand-resort-as-hunting-lodge style similar to the Awahnee in Yellowstone. Under timbered roofs sprawls furniture as oversized as the fireplace, and the benign gaze of mounted wildlife (whether now politically correct or not, Teddy Roosevelt contributed a few of the animal trophies) surveys the lobby. If the rugged gentility is gracious any time, it is lavish over the holidays, right down to Santa hats on the antlered guardians on walls garnished with garlands.

In summer, rocking chairs line the porches. But now we all duck in through the heavy door quickly, choosing instead a couch by the blazing hearth or maybe a chair in the cozy lounge with a brandy to help take off the chill. Stopping at Yavapai Overlook on the way up to photograph the scene in snow, I was pleased at how mild the temperature seemed — until I turned to come back. The wind chill blasted my face into numbness. But safe in the lobby, it seems fun again.

El Tovar forms the perfect counterpoint to nature's harshness. That's probably always one of its greatest appeals. You can hike the Bright Angel Trail. Train until your calves burn and are covered in red dust, then appropriate one of the chairs on the lounge patio and drink something very full of ice, partaking of the best of civilization on the heels of the best of the wilderness. To have a waiter pour steaming coffee from a sterling pot while you behold deer nibbling around outside the long windows enhances both.

And after raising your heart rate by climbing the steep stairs from the depot, or throwing snow on the lawn, the warmth and comfort of deep carpet and a conversationally snapping fire give yin to your yang.

Perhaps the only reason to wait for Christmas is the holiday dinner. Chef Joseph Noble and pastry Chef Joan Chaffee have worked the menu out in advance. Reading about apple-smoked pork loin with rum-raisin glaze, roasted sweet potatoes, and baby green beans, followed by eggnog cheesecake, who wouldn't want to stay? But even before the holiday rush, the pine boughs, ribbon garlands, and a gingerbread fantasy are already in place, and the allure of having the place virtually to oneself is grand. Besides, the everyday menu, which Chef Joseph says he and Chef Joan get to update annually, is a symphony of sensational offerings. (Our son, having finished a simple macaroni and cheese that surpassed all prior, gave the dining room "five thumbs up and 10 stars.") So while we had to miss the chili-rubbed salmon tostada with pico de gallo, citrus rice, and fire-roasted corn salsa, the artichoke chicken and rich gorgonzola mashed potatoes made up for everything.

Chef Joseph said the dining room will provide 600 meals Christmas Day, while the weeks before and after the holiday are the quietest of the year. (On Thanksgiving Day, and peak summer weekends, they may serve 1,200 meals.) He and Chef Joan share tidbits of gourmet discoveries made while at El Tovar (they started as interns here in 1994). One is that dark chocolate is a universal favorite, while white chocolate desserts have as many foes as friends. Another truism: No matter how scrumptious a raspberry chocolate mousse cake with truffle cream might be, on Thanksgiving, everyone goes for the desserts with pumpkin and pecan. Chef Joan is the architect of the mansions of gingerbread, meticulously decorated with a benevolence of sweets. Individual gingerfolk can even be taken home at the end of the holiday.

If there is a special imperative to coming up over Christmas, it is that the expectant stillness of the season seems in a perfect setting here. To see the year-round resident ravens still on patrol, watch the panoply of shadow play, with the added attractions of frost and fog and falling snow, is to be able to absorb the quiet wonder that is always present in the world, but which we can lose sight of in the inflated schedules we inflict on ourselves.

Our room, with the classical furnishings and elegant appointments, welcomes us back after an evening session listening to ghost stories by the big fireplace after dinner. (A word to the wise — they may be too vividly told and easy to imagine for young children or for the young at heart.)

Before succumbing to the siren lure of snuggling under comforters, it's impossible to resist one more look out at what brings us all here: the silent, timeless Canyon itself, which has continued to change and charm and inspire since long before there was any reason for Christmas. Looking at starlit silence unpunctuated by people, while cosseted and nurtured by the hospitable arms of the grand old lodge, it is easier to believe in the possibility of peace on earth.

yon he comes

52

As the year ends, the night sky always reminds me of John Thomas.

He was the janitor at KGUN-TV in Tucson long before the term "maintenance engineer" had been coined. My father and I both worked at KGUN, but John Thomas started there before either of us. I remember holiday parties when I was a child, and my dad a new employee, seeing the Thomas girls all wide-eyed and shy, staying close together in their rustly, big-skirted dresses and shiny shoes. I wore those also, but was fascinated by their hair, corn-rowed or pigtailed in bright ribbons.

Who knows what wonders the night sky might hide.

DECEMBER

241

John beamed with pride at what he called "my little crumb-crushers. Ooo-ee, ain't they fine!"

John's drawl lingered from his Texas childhood. He went back to visit come summer, and my dad always delighted in asking John the name of his home town, because the answer tickled him.

"I'm goin' home to Woofsie, Texas," John Thomas would say with relish.

My father kind of spoiled it once by opening an atlas and asking where exactly Woofsie lay on the map. After a quick scan, John pointed to Wolfe City. But to us, it's still Woofsie.

John was also a great Bible-verse man and knew my father for a kindred soul, raised in Sunday School competitions. When the two met in the hall, John might lean on his broom, eyes bright with anticipation. "All, right, Mistah Larry, how about 'Blessed are those who grieve . . . '" he would challenge.

John Thomas wanted people to be happy, and in his mind my dad couldn't really achieve that happiness without grandchildren. So when I was a reporter there, if he found me in the coffee room, he would generally ask when I was going to give Mistah Larry some grandbabies.

"Soon as I can, John," I would say. He wasn't pushy. He just liked things right in the world, and to him that meant me settled down and producing grandbabies for his friend.

There were times I sensed John Thomas tired of playing the role he had chosen, of the genial get-along guy greeting everyone with a smile. The veneer slipped only once that I saw, when he was describing a man who had cheated him out of a month's wages as a caretaker. Then his eyes narrowed and his voice got hard. It was like seeing Santa roll his own cigarette. My surprise must have shown, for he quickly adapted his features back to the jolly, comforting norm.

"It's not what I'd'a wished, Miss Lisa," he said, "but it's what the Good Lord a'chose for me, and that's the best thing."

I wanted to tell him he didn't have to be in character all the time, but

I was afraid to make him uncomfortable. He'd probably grown up where survival in a white man's world meant staying true to a certain role.

By this time John Thomas was in his 80s and still spry and early to work, each day dressed in a freshly pressed striped shirt with his name embroidered over the pocket. He courted a widow lady from his church and rolled his eyes describing her savory dinners. Every Christmas my parents looked forward to getting a section of Miss Laureen's special sweet potato pie.

But then one year, it didn't come; the first sign of things not right. John had slipped and fallen just before Christmas and ended up in the hospital.

For the first time, he wasn't master of his small but loyal and well-run universe. Realizing how quickly he went from being in charge to being helpless took all the sass and vinegar out of John. He went from the hospital to a nursing home near the TV station. Nursing homes don't bother me as much as some people, so I tried to get over there whenever I could.

One evening after work I dropped by, and Ken Dillon was there. He was our chief photographer, and I found out he and John went to the same gospel church. John Thomas was giving Ken a good scolding for not making it to choir practice any more.

"You ought to be ashamed of yo'self, letting down your mama that way! A fine woman like her, can't hold up her head in singin' cause her boy's too important and busy to come!" They were joshing each other, and John looked pretty bright.

I had brought a little old artificial Christmas tree. A bit flattened, it showed more space than branches, but I knew ornaments and lights would make it cheerful. Ken, who could be moody but was comfortable and congenial, helped me put it up.

Upbraiding Ken must have taken the end of the day's energy, for John drifted off to sleep just after I arrived. So Ken and I decorated the little tree. John looked small in the white bed, without his glasses.

"He wants to die, he says," Ken told me, shaking his head. That surprised me, and scared me — the station wouldn't feel right without John, and I had heard too many stories of people giving up on life to think his attitude wouldn't make a powerful difference in his recovery.

Standing with Ken, looking at this man we both cared for, felt surprisingly like family. The teasing and decorating and talking were what families do, and it felt like families can be set up anywhere, like Bedouin tents. Or corrals. Or Christmas trees.

The next time I went to see John, he was alone, and pretty sad. He told me then that he wanted to die.

"I want to see them pearly gates," he said, gripping my hand with an intensity that implied I had connections and could get him what he wanted.

I'd never actually heard someone refer to "them pearly gates" before. I told him we didn't get to choose when we went, but knew he would do what he could to lobby for immediate departure.

Perhaps to remind him of some pleasures existed in this world, I asked if he thought much about Woofsie. It got him reminiscing about the swimming hole on Ol' Man Someone's property, where the boys would sneak in during hot summer days to go skinny-dipping.

"Cep' one of us had to be lookout for the old man," he said. "Everything'd be right as rain, playin' and cold, till Ol' Man was spotted. Then the lookout would commence to shout, 'Yon he comes! Yon he comes! And everyone'd scatter and grab gear and go," John said. He closed his eyes, and I sat fascinated. I could see them splashing, boisterous and free in the sunny water, till the alert. And I could see the scurrying boy's memories still lived behind the old man's eyes.

That was the last time I saw John Thomas. He died a few nights later. His son was with him.

He'd earned the right; lived a good life and treated people well. It would take some getting used to, having him gone. When I left work that night, I looked up at the sky, bright with stars visible even in the city. For the first time, I wanted there to be actual pearly gates some-where. Shining up there, beyond those stars, that you could touch with your hand.

So John Thomas would know it was all worth it. So he'd know his preacher had told it exactly right.

So he could look up and see those tall pretty gates swing open, and see the Almighty Himself, waiting for ol' John Thomas with a smile as big as Texas, in wonder and rightness.

Yon he comes, Lord. Yon he comes.

index

Oak Creek flows within easy view from Los Abrigados Resort.

Chief Yellowhorse's billboard on U.S. Route 89 has a message for any who didn't stop at a nearby shop.